reaching
new heights

through kindness
in marriage

Also by Miriam Yerushalmi

For Adults (Forthcoming)

Reaching New Heights Through Kindness In Prayer

Reaching New Heights Through Inner Peace And Happiness

Reaching New Heights Through Full Immersion

Reaching New Heights Tefilah Cards

Reaching New Heights Marriage Cards

Reaching New Heights Happiness Cards

Reaching New Heights Mikvah Cards

Reaching New Heights Marriage Workbook

For Children (Available)

Feivel the Falafel Ball Who Wanted to Do a *Mitzvah**

Gedalia the Goldfish Who Wanted to Be Like the King*

Let's Go Camping and Discover Our Nature

Beautiful Like a *Kallah*

Carrying a Tune in *Tzefat*

The Best Dressed*

Color My Day the Jewish Way

Castle Around My Heart

Let's Go to Eretz Yisrael*

*Also in Yiddish

reaching
new heights

through kindness
in marriage

by miriam yerushalmi M.A. M.S.

ISBN-13: 9781934152423 | ISBN-10: 1-934152-42-0

© Copyright 2017 by Miriam Yerushalmi

Published *Torah For Life*, Brooklyn, NY. torahfl@gmail.com

Contact the author at: miriamyerushalmi18@gmail.com

First Edition — 2017.

Cover illustration by Shoshana Brombacher

Chapter 10 appeared in The Jewish Press Supplement May 28th, 2014 in a slightly revised form, under the title Compassionate Parenting: The Secret to Healthy and Successful Children, by Miriam Yerushalmi, MS and Chana Kaiman, LCSW.

All quotes from the Five Books of the Chumash are with permission from the Gutnick Edition, translation and commentary by Rabbi Chaim Miller (New York: Kol Menachem, 2008).

With gratitude to

Rabbi Chaim Miller

for laboring over

this book

and for assisting with

its publication.

Contents

Testimonials

"Miriam Yerushalmi is an astounding therapist who has been working for two years with SPARKS, an organization I am very close with which helps women with perinatal depression. She is devoted to helping women in need and is successful in treating them. I believe her book *Reaching New Heights* has a lot of knowledge to offer and will be an inspiring read to all."

—Rabbi Dr. Abraham J. Twerski

"Miriam Yerushalmi has a deep understanding and a broad knowledge of Chasidic literature and she uses it effectively to heal souls. In this volume she shares that wisdom delicately with you, in a way that transforms you and your marriage."

—Rabbi Chaim Miller

"Mrs Miriam Yerushalmi presents a unique approach which is a beautiful blend of her Chassidic insight and her understanding of human nature. Her ability to see things from a deeper perspective enables her to guide young men and women into improving their personal lives and their marriage in the most challenging of situations. Her determination to keep the family together no matter what, is refreshing in a time when people are getting professional advice in a very different direction."

"The women that I referred to Miriam for counseling were grateful."

—Rabbi Shloma Majesky

"This book helps connect the seemingly disconnected dots that allow for a clearer picture of you, yourself, your relationships and ultimately, a clearer picture of your best life."

—Judith Leventhal, C.S.W., author *Small Miracles*

"Miriam Yerushalmi is a very successful therapist and an expert on meditation. A part of the SPARKS team, she has conducted deep meditations for women healing from Postpartum Depression and similar mood disorders, enabling them to rebuild their self-image and reconcile past traumas. Her meditations and talks are part of the SPARKS Audio Library, where thousands connect for self-help.

—Esther Kenigsberg, SPARKS founder and president

"Miriam has freely shared her prolific educational and spiritual materials with *Jewish Girls Unite* and she has been a guest presenter at retreats and online. The girls gained a whole new appreciation for prayer and meditation. This book is an incredible resource to inspire yourself, as well as to teach others the tools to love and appreciate the gift of prayer."

—Nechama Laber, *Jewish Girls Unite*

From Miriam's Clients

The following testimonials were transcribed by Yaacov Dovid Shulman from audio tapes recorded by my clients, and accurately express their words and sentiments. May these stories give hope to others who want to follow these paths as a bridge to happiness.

1. "I No Longer See Anything Dark in My Life"

I started receiving counseling from Miriam because I had a lot of anger towards my children and my husband. With Miriam's help, I have been learning to be kind to my husband and my children in both my thoughts and words. Before, I was never really able to feel grateful for what I had.

But now, when I wake up in the morning, the first thing I do is recite the *modeh ani*—"I give thanks to Hashem." I am grateful for my husband, for my children, for my house, for the weather. I no longer see anything dark in my life.

My mother told me that she can't believe that I'm the same person I used to be, because I've changed so much. I said, "Mom, I didn't change. This is the real me coming out." She said, "I don't remember you being like this since you were seven or eight. You were an angry person as a child and you have been so angry at your children, your husband, everybody."

All of these changes happened since my learning with Miriam. She gave me her marriage book to read and advised me to meditate and pray. I feel very good. I feel that no medication can do what all of this has done for me. Now I can control my emotions. In regard to my relationship with my husband, I started working on myself and as I changed, he changed too. He did not even meet with Miriam.

Also, my son has changed so much that I cannot even recognize him. In the past, he would always wake up in a bad mood. Now the first thing he does is run to me, hug me and say, "Good morning, Mom." A few days ago, when my mom visited us, my son embraced her and said "Hi, welcome." She was amazed. "He has never come and hugged me." Last year my son's school would call me every day to complain about him. This year, *baruch Hashem*, I haven't gotten one such call. Recently, he called me from school to say that he had forgotten his baseball mitt at home, and he asked me to bring it to him. I told him that I was busy and couldn't do it. Last year he would have screamed and cried that I'm not fair, and hung up the phone. But this time he just said, "OK, Mommy, I understand."

The whole atmosphere in the house has improved. My husband used to complain that he comes to a home where everybody is screaming and crying. Last night, I opened the door to him with a big smile because I had had a good day. I had received good news that my children are doing well at school. I embraced him, kissed him and sang *heiveinu shalom aleichem*, and I started dancing. My children were so happy to see this. When they see me shining, then they shine as well. It's a circle. I will give one more example. I have always hated the rain and whenever rain fell, I would feel very sad. But recently, rain fell for two days in a row, and it didn't affect me. I felt happy. I cannot recognize myself any more. It's wonderful.

2. "Now My Marriage Is Really Working Out for the Better"

I am grateful to Hashem for introducing me to Miriam. She is such a great soul. I went through many crises in my marriage, and I wanted to get a divorce. There was so much anger and rage. There was so much fighting and I was always so sad. I met Miriam at one of her lectures, and the rest is history. I started to come regularly to her classes and she gave me some extra time after the classes to learn how to pray with the specific meditations of how to control my negative emotions. Now my marriage is really working out for the better, and I love my husband more. Miriam taught me not to be needy but to think about what my husband needs. She taught me to be a giver, to look at my husband's actions positively, to forgive and forget, and to tell him what I need instead of blaming him when I lack something. First and foremost, she taught me the importance of connecting myself to Hashem and bringing Him into my life in everything that I do.

3. "I Am No Longer Controlled by Negative Thoughts or Impulses"

Three years ago, I received a diagnosis of bipolar disorder. Medicine helped me maintain some normalcy and stay somewhat functional, but it couldn't cure the disease. So I was always swinging from being too "up" to being too "down." I paid hundreds of thousands of dollars out-of-pocket for medical help that didn't help me, and I went to psychotherapists for two years, which only made me feel worse. During this time I got married, and within a year my husband and I were having such serious problems that I was almost ready to get a divorce.

At this point, I started to see Miriam Yerushalmi. She taught me that it is important for my soul to be able to sit inside my body, and to that end I have to make myself a vessel for God's light. She taught me to learn through three things: *hisbonenus* meditation, working on myself spiritually and keeping all the laws of the Torah, such as the laws of family purity (*taharas hamishpachah*) and *kashrus*. I started to learn some Torah, listen to Jewish music, and guard my eyes and ears. I learned to humble myself in a way that I'm confident and know that everything is from God.

The most important lesson that I learned (which was the biggest trigger point of change for me) was how to be happy no matter what. Being happy enables a person to overcome anything. Once you're only accustomed to be positive, you're completely different. Less than three months after I started to learn from Miriam and connect to what she knows, I started to feel straightened out. All of a sudden, my brain started to work. Now I feel healthier and focused. I am no longer controlled by negative thoughts or impulses. It is such an amazing experience to feel clarity and not have weird thoughts. My brain has started to slow down and feel relaxed.

This is something that no medicine, no doctors, no therapist, was able to give me.

4. "Our Marriage Is Loving Instead of Filled with Tension and Hatred"

Miriam Yerushalmi was tremendously effective in improving my marriage. My relationship with my husband was extremely explosive. Just as a car can go from zero to a hundred kilometers an hour in one minute, my husband and I might be sitting quietly at the dinner table and the next moment we would explode over something trivial— often before our children and grandchildren. We consulted psychiatrist after psychiatrist. What I learned from all of the therapists was that I have to show my husband that he has to treat me like an equal. But the more I tried to do this, the more he would push back to show me that what he says goes.

And so things only went from bad to worse. At that point, I started taking Miriam Yerushalmi's classes and I would consult with her after her classes. Everything started to change when she said to me, "There's a lot of fire in your husband." She explained to me about the four elements (fire, water, air, and earth) of the animal soul and how one element may be more dominant in one person than it is in another. All of a sudden I realized that she's right. That is his character. I realized that I shouldn't take the things he does personally. If he has a lot of fire in him, what I have to do is not add fuel to the fire by talking back, yelling, disagreeing and demanding to be treated as his equal. Instead, I should do things diplomatically, with tact—I should be a wife the Torah way.

Miriam taught me how to be calm, how to control my words and not speak when I'm angry. That itself was itself a whole new way of life for me. And she taught me to daven with more feeling, to do *hitbonenut* meditation, to give charity, to do teshuvah every night before going to bed.

She taught me that when we have peace in the home, G-d's Presence lives among us, and when we don't, His Presence leaves. And her stories brought everything to life and drove home her points in a beautiful way that inspired me to act.

My husband never went to any meetings or classes with Miriam. He doesn't know her at all. But the more I changed, the more he changed. The more I showed him that we're a team, that I'm his team member, that I'm on his side— instead of my previous combative, confrontational attitude— the nicer and more loving he acted. Everything that Miriam taught me brought my husband and me back to loving each other. Now our marriage is loving instead of filled with tension and hatred. The change in our relationship is like the difference between night and day.

5. "Miriam Gave Me the Techniques to Change My Family Around"

I was having a difficult time with my husband, who was drunk and abusive, and with my children. Miriam gave me the techniques to change my family around. My husband is no longer drunk and abusive, and my children are better off. Miriam has always been available, and everything she says has really helped. Without her, our lives wouldn't be the same.

6. "My Whole Life Changed"

When I was growing up, my parents, brothers and sisters abused me and even hit me. I learned not to say anything and to accept the abuse. After I married, that pattern continued. My husband, mother-in-law, sister-in-law and others mistreated me, and I didn't tell them to stop. And when they saw that I didn't defend myself, they continued doing so.

I grew so depressed that my life became unbearable. I went to therapists and spoke with my rabbi, and they advised me to get a divorce. During this time, many people told me that I have to forgive. I really wanted to do so, with all my heart, but I couldn't. I didn't know how. At that point, I started to see Miriam Yerushalmi. She listened to me, understood me and helped me, and as a result my depression left.

The first thing that she taught me was how to strengthen myself through praying and meditating so that I wouldn't let what other people do depress me. She taught me that the most important way for me to defend myself was to calmly tell someone who is abusing me to stop. But the most important thing that I learned from Miriam was how to forgive. I learned that if somebody is doing bad things to me, instead of hating them, I should change my feelings and perceptions. For instance, I should feel sorry for her.

When I learned how to forgive, my whole life changed. In particular, this lesson changed my marriage. I started everything from the beginning with my husband, exactly as if we had just gotten married. Miriam also talked to my husband, and his behavior improved. Miriam also taught me to pray and trust in Hashem. And she gave me meditations, which really help. I regularly meditate for everything that I want. Even before I go to sleep, I meditate. In particular, this helps me forgive. Now I have a happy home. Thank you, Hashem!

7. "Miriam Gave Me Back My Hope"

On the advice of our rabbis and *mashpi'im* (spiritual advisers), my spouse and I were divorced. Some time later, a friend of mine went to Miriam Yerushalmi and suggested that she help us get back together. She phoned me a number of times, but I argued that the rabbis had counseled that we get a divorce and I refused to consider her help.

Finally, I started going to Miriam to receive her support and counsel; however, I didn't change my mind about the divorce. Then one day, about five months after I had started working with Miriam, I saw my former spouse on the street, walking in my direction. We started talking, and we agreed that about eighty per cent of the time our marriage had been good. I said, "If that's the case, then maybe Miriam Yerushalmi could help us out."

After this meeting, I realized how special my spouse was to me: the only one for me, my soul mate without whom I couldn't get along, and with whom I wanted to share my life forever.

I found myself crying. I davened to Hashem more often and more deeply than ever before. I would write letters to deliver to the Rebbe's *ohel* ("tent," or gravesite). Sometimes I screamed aloud in my apartment. I was empty in an empty house, all by myself, with nobody to talk to. I couldn't fall sleep at night and I would lie awake in bed until six in the morning.

But my former spouse refused to consider our remarrying. I spent a year trying to figure out how to get back together again. I spoke to Miriam Yerushalmi and worked together with her. I read her book, I listened to her CDs, I used her meditations and I consulted with her, in person and on the telephone. Miriam gave me back my hope. She gave me a positive outlook on how to feel good about myself and about my ex, and helped me to feel hopeful about the prospect of our getting back together again.

In the meantime, my ex and I slowly started dating, until we finally decided to get married again....

It is important to me to know that Miriam Yerushalmi is always available to help me. She has been a source of inspiration and has shown me the right path. Miriam's way of delving into *Chassidus*, with her woman's touch, has helped and shown me how to come closer to Hashem and, with His help, have a wonderful marriage.

8. "My Daughter Is Now on a Journey of Growth and Accomplishment"

Psychotherapy tries to solve a person's problems by uncovering and repairing his past traumas. And so when I went to psychotherapists to help me deal with my daughter's issues, they told me that I first had to solve problems from my own childhood. But I didn't have the time!

During this period, I began attending Miriam Yerushalmi's *Tanya* classes. I learned from her that *Chassidus* works on repairing the soul in the present through teshuvah, which changes the past and opens up a person's power to change. I discovered that I got more out of attending one such class than I did from a whole year in psychotherapy. The improvements I experienced were immediate and life-changing.

My attending Miriam's classes has helped me be slower to anger, to watch my words and respond in a more refined way toward my children and my husband. I began seeing Miriam for private sessions as well to help me deal with my daughter and my other children, and also to improve my marital relationship.

Miriam has also worked directly with my daughter and my other children.

After my daughter learned with Miriam on a weekly basis for just a few months, she surprised us by bringing home a glowing report card, reflecting her huge improvements in conduct, learning and grades. She also had many friends come to bring *shalach manos* on Purim and calling to get together with her to play – more than ever before, *Baruch Hashem!*

My daughter's learning *Chassidus* with Miriam Yerushalmi has made her happier with herself and taught her that she has the power to change for the better in all areas of her life, at home and at school. She is now on a journey of personal growth and accomplishment. I have seen tremendous change for the better. Her grades, her concentration, her enthusiasm for learning and her social skills have all improved.

On days that my daughter falls a bit, I can always call Miriam for encouragement or listen to some of her shiurim on the phone together with the whole family. Miriam has even walked over to my home to spend time with my daughter when my daughter has had a hard day.

Miriam cares about all of my children as though they are her own. She takes each child under her wings to educate them in the ways of *Chassidus* and help them conquer their *yetzer hara* by creating a proper vessel for their Godly soul through learning, prayer, meditation, singing *nigunim* and giving charity. She teaches these concepts on a level that my children can understand—in a fun, creative way through music, dance, and drama.

As for my marriage, before getting Miriam's guidance, I had experienced tension and confusion. After learning with Miriam, I have gained hope and encouragement, because I now realize how much depends on me, and I have the tools to make small and yet drastic changes and improvements in my marriage. Miriam has taught me that much of a good marriage depends on the wife demonstrating respect for her husband. When she sees her husband stumble she should respond with kindness (and sometimes silence!). In that way, she has the power to change her husband, her marriage, and even her children for the better.

Hashem has given Miriam the gift of healing by using the tools of *Tanya* and *Chassidus* to help us become the best that we can be.

9. "Miriam Yerushalmi is a G-d-sent presence"

Miriam Yerushalmi is a G-d-sent presence who has helped me and so many others have *shalom bayit*. I have studied with her, and through her help and guidance was able to achieve a loving and harmonious relationship with my husband. A few years ago, things were so difficult between me and my husband that I was in total despair, and felt that my marriage could not be salvaged. Miriam helped me through this very difficult time, and I was able to restore my love and respect for my husband and learn to recognize and accept his imperfections as well as my own flaws. I learned to be less judgmental and more appreciative of the good things that my husband has brought into our marriage. I am thankful that today I have managed to feel a new-found respect for my husband. I can also feel his growing love and respect for me.

Marriage is a two-way street: in order to gain love, one must learn how to give unconditional love with patience and good cheer. Happiness and a loving heart are the ingredients to bring a loving spark into all of our relationships in this journey called life.

Miriam, thank you for your help and guidance! May you be blessed to bring warmth, love and comfort to all of our Jewish families.

Preface

The Sunday of my first visit to the Chabad Lubavitch community of Crown Heights happened to fall on *Lag B'Omer,* the day which marks a happy milestone in the seven-week *sefirah* period extending from Pesach (Passover) to Shavuos (Tabernacles, the Festival of Weeks). A public celebration of the day was taking place in the women's section of the main synagogue, 770 Eastern Parkway. An enormous gathering of mothers together with their small children was enjoying the festive atmosphere.

In just over two weeks we would be celebrating the holiday of Shavuos, on which the Jewish people re-live the experience of receiving the Torah. Our Sages tell us that the souls of every Jew, even past and future, were present at the foot of Mt. Sinai when G-d gave us the Torah. I knew no one in the large crowd around me, yet I felt close to each woman, as though our souls had indeed been together before.

Our Sages teach that on Shavuos, Hashem was our bridegroom, we were His bride, and the Torah was the *kesubah*, the marriage contract. It was a time of immeasurable holiness and happiness. Our own wedding day may have mirrored that experience. Such moments of holy awareness, of rapturous feeling, are precious and rare. How can we keep them alive when we return to the routine of everyday life, which tends to undermine our sense of spirituality? Moreover, how can we do so if our marriage is not the blissful partnership we envisioned at the outset?

As a teacher and a marriage and family counselor for almost 30 years, I have encountered many individuals who have been struggling with issues that threaten their *shalom bayis*, the peace and harmony in the home. Generally, their problems are common, but most of them do not realize it. Rather, they think that the challenges that they face are unusual, and as a result they feel isolated and hopeless. Whether they are newlyweds or married for over fifty years, they voice variations on the same theme: "I made such a big mistake," "We are such opposites it isn't funny," and "We are a great match. I drive him crazy and he makes me sick!"

Many of these individuals or couples have tried traditional marriage counseling, yet found that it didn't help or that it even made things worse. With the mounting number of such cases, I realized that there was a need for a book that can teach people the skills necessary to cope with the normal challenges that arise when two people with different personalities, backgrounds, and predispositions join together to form the most intimate of human relationships: marriage.

My approach draws heavily on the teachings of Rabbi Shneur Zalman of Liadi, the first Rebbe of Chabad (1745-1812) and his book known as *Tanya*, as well as the teachings of Rabbi Menachem Mendel Schneerson, the Lubavitcher Rebbe.

As a child, I was amazed at how difficult it seemed for people to change their negative character traits. Human beings are certainly able to exercise more control than this, I thought. Later in life, when I was attending college, I was attracted to the study of psychology because it offered the promise of answering this question. In particular, I thought that by studying psychology I would be able to find the keys to controlling my emotions and that I would then be able to help others do so as well.

But even years after I completed my degrees, I was still searching for the answers to my original questions. My logic told me that Hashem did not create human beings without the ability to control their emotions, so I prayed to Him to lead me to the answers, and I continued to search.

My prayers were answered. G-d led me to teachers who introduced me to the inner dimensions of the Torah: those parts of *Chassidic* philosophy, including its mystical elements that address the question of man's purpose in the world and provide the keys to achieving a life of harmony, joy, and self-mastery.

Initially, I experimented by applying this newfound knowledge to my own spiritual and personal growth. These techniques proved to be so useful that I could hardly wait to share them with others. I have been fortunate to be able to do so over the course of my career through my CDs, books, classes and private practice as a counselor.

I have consistently found that these techniques help people achieve more fulfilling marriages, self-mastery, and a greater level of joy in their service of Hashem.

Living according to the teachings of *Chassidus* has changed my life for the better. I am humbled that with the help of *Hakadosh Baruch Hu* (G-d, the Holy One, may He be blessed), it has enabled me to help others as well.

This book is my humble effort to fulfill the Rebbe's request that all Jews help married couples, as expressed in the following letter.[1]

Greetings and blessings,

Your letter reached me with some delay. Thank you very much also for the enclosures dealing with your activities and programs.

I hope that you are making efforts not only to maintain your activities in high gear, but also to extend them from time to time. For, needless to say, a marriage in Jewish life is an institution which is called a "binyan adei ad, an everlasting edifice." And in order that it should be so, it is necessary that everything connected with marriage of a bride and groom should

_____

1

be in full compliance with the instructions of our Torah, which is called "Toras Chayim, [living Torah]" because it is not only the source of everlasting life in the Hereafter, but also the true guide in life on this earth.

The analogy of a marriage to an "everlasting edifice" is not merely a figure of speech, but there is an important idea and instruction in it. It is that just as in the case of any structure, the first and most important thing is to ensure the quality and durability of the foundation, lacking which all the efforts put into the walls and roof and decorations, etc., would be of no avail. And so it is in regard to a Jewish marriage which, first of all, must be based on the foundation of the Torah and mitzvos; then follows the blessing of the joy and rejoicing of the beloved couple for the rest of their life.

In view of the above, it is also clear that there is a standing obligation upon everyone to help a bride and groom to establish such an everlasting edifice, and it would be totally unjustified to think that it is a matter of their own personal life, in which no one has the right to interfere. Surely when one sees someone bent on harming herself or himself and their children, or about to do something which might lead to self-destruction, G-d forbid, one will not consider it "interference" or "encroachment" to try to prevent that harm [from occurring]. Similarly, when there is an opportunity to help someone with a lasting benefit, surely it is one's elementary duty to do so. How much more [pressing is that duty] when the benefit is a truly everlasting one!

I send you my prayerful wishes to continue your good work in helping young couples to establish Jewish homes—homes that are illuminated with the light of the Torah and mitzvos, *and above all with the observance of the laws and regulations of Taharas Hamishpacha (Family Purity)*, and that you do so with deep inspiration and with ever-growing success.*

(Rabbi Menachem Mendel Schneerson, Letters from the Rebbe (Brooklyn: Otsar Sifrei Lubavitch, 1998-2005), vol. 2, pp. 48-50.)

*Please note that in this book, we do not address the subject of *Taharas Hamishpacha* in depth, even though it is an essential element in building a true Jewish home. We do include a selection of related *kavanot* (see Appendix). There are many fine books and other resources already available on this topic, such as "Total Immersion," edited by Rivkah Slonim; "Bread, Fire, and Water" by Rabbi A. Silberger, and the books and lectures of Rebbetzin Sarah Karmely. See also my forthcoming booklet on the *Mikvah* experience.

Introduction

This book is meant for everyone. The information and strategies that it provides were tested over the past three decades in my work as a marriage and family counselor. They have helped couples preparing for marriage as well as married couples whose relationships were at risk. Moreover, they have helped strengthen happy marriages. As the Lubavitcher Rebbe often said, "Good is good, but better is better."

Marriage can be as holy as a "devouring fire," full of fervor, passion, and enthusiasm. Each can connect with the other and become attached with a bond so strong, to feel so beloved by the other and feel such a love for the other, that their unity creates within them the most eternal peace on earth, an internal serenity that manifests externally in all their ways.

This true love experience ignites a soul ascent, eager to capture the rapture of Oneness; unifying each other wherever they might be, near or far, always close in heart and soul, until together they are able to conquer worlds, to make an abode for divinity here on earth; to build a true Jewish home out of that beautiful love, a miniature sanctuary of their own.

I pray as you read this book that you see the holiness in yourselves and in your spouse, that you experience much delight all the days of your life, forever TOGETHER, reaching new heights.

Even husbands and wives who feel that something is amiss in their marriages can reach these heights. Perhaps the relationship has no major conflict, but it just is not the bastion of companionship, warmth, and security each spouse had dreamed of. Over time, a relationship may become characterized by lashing out and defensive reactions as husband and wife, instead of building a "bayis ne'eman" together, erect emotional walls to hide behind or to keep the other out. All too often, this behavior leads a couple to resign themselves to an unhappy or unfulfilling marriage.

Under such circumstances it is difficult enough to maintain love of self, let alone maintain feelings of love for a spouse, who is seen as exacerbating one's pain, if not the source of it.

How did two people who together have the potential for G-dliness fall into such a situation? More importantly, how can peace and love develop in homes and hearts that are surrounded by negativity?

Simply put, the answer to the latter questions is, "with kindness." Kindness is the bridge over which you can travel from pain to peace, from shouting to shalom. Kindness can bridge any distance between you and your spouse, or between you and the person you wish to be. Treating yourself, your spouse, and the others in your life with kindness is the first and most important step toward saving your relationships.

This book is designed to teach you the strategies to achieve and build on this vital trait. It will describe the work that you can do to improve the way you relate to your spouse, your children, and Hashem. You will also learn how to enable your physical self to live in more harmony with your soul.

By practicing the techniques described in this book, you will be empowered to transcend your ego and counter the negative internal messages that undermine your G-d-given capabilities. When you feel tension in your marriage, instead of yielding to feelings of negativity and hopelessness, you will know how to work to reveal your love for yourself, for Hashem, and for the others in your life. The benefits will spill over to non-family relationships as well.

In his book *The Chassidic Approach to Joy*, Rabbi Shloma Majeski tells a story about Rabbi Yechezkel Feigen, a *mashpia* (spiritual guide) in the Lubavitcher *yeshiva* in Russia during the 1920s:

In those days, religious gatherings were prohibited and punishable with incarceration in a labor camp. And so a yeshiva student would always be appointed as a watchman to warn of approaching government agents.

Once, during a farbrengen (gathering), Rabbi Feigen urged his students to make a deeper commitment to prayer, study, and character development. He spoke with such a fiery intensity, directing the students to the specific areas where they needed to concentrate their efforts, that many of them were literally moved to tears.

Suddenly, the watchman came running in with the news that the Russian secret police were searching the area. The students jumped into action, one urging that they try to flee, another that they turn off the lights, and a third suggesting that they scatter newspapers and political science books around to make it appear as if they were involved in government-approved activities.

As it turned out, the secret police left the area as abruptly as they had come, without even entering the building. Rabbi Feigen and his students were able to sit down to resume the farbrengen. Rabbi Feigen then asked the students, "Why, when I spoke about your spiritual well-being, did you all cry, but when you heard that the OGPU was in the area and your lives were in danger, nobody cried?"

Puzzled, one of the students replied, "We had to figure out a way to save ourselves. There was no time to cry!"

"I see," the rabbi responded. "To save your physical selves, you knew that crying wouldn't help and you had to act. Yet why when it comes to spiritual matters is it acceptable to cry and do nothing else?"

Rabbi Feigin repeated this concept until the students understood that crying can be used as a means of avoiding action. A person who is serious about making changes in his life does not have time to cry. Every moment is precious and can be used to implement a solution.

Apply this concept to the issues you face in your marriage. Refrain from sinking into sadness over your situation. You have the ability to effect positive changes in your life! Begin now to take the steps necessary to improve your situation. Begin your walk over the bridge of kindness, to a better marriage.

In this book I share many of the teachings of the great Chabad luminaries Rabbi Shneur Zalman of Liadi and Rabbi Menachem Mendel Schneerson, the Lubavitcher Rebbe, and other Torah sources I employ in conjunction with practical techniques to improve a marriage. Some of the solutions I present may seem simple, and you may at first think that you do not need to read this book, because you already know them. But it is good to review such material. In addition, you will likely find—as have many of my clients over the years—that simple changes, such as smiling more often, can have amazing positive effects.

I hope that after reading this book and internalizing its message, you will be able to clear your mind of unhelpful ideas about marriage that you may have absorbed from the popular culture, and strengthen your commitment to achieving *shalom bayis*.

It is recommended that you read the book from beginning to end and do all of the exercises and visualizations, which will help you respond appropriately to real-life challenges. If you find at any point that a passage is too difficult, simply skip it and return to it later on. Then read the book again in order to better absorb the information.

(Note: It is critical to state that anyone undergoing emotional or psychiatric difficulties may need medical treatment, especially if there is any danger to oneself or others. Once stabilized, if the person can become focused and receptive, work can begin on improving their marriage, while following doctor's orders regarding medical care.

Bear in mind, though, that modern science cannot heal everything. A disorder may result from spiritual factors, and I have seen this often. The Lubavitcher Rebbe wrote a number of letters to physicians in which he pointed out the need for people to pay attention to the spiritual elements affecting both their physical and mental health. In such cases the spiritual factors must of course be addressed.)

In this book, I often quote from other books and teachers whose wisdom I have found helpful in my marriage and in my work. Almost all of the ideas herein have been culled from the commentaries and insights of the great *Chassidic* masters. I am, however, solely responsible for any errors that may have inadvertently crept into this book and I am also solely responsible for the actual selection of the ideas and comments of others that I have chosen to include.

May this book dramatically enrich the quality of your marriage!

Dear Reader,

A note before you read this book. My goal in writing this books is to present to you a Jewish perspective of why we sometimes encounter difficulties in our lives.

This book—based upon my classes and my counseling sessions—is about what we can do to keep ourselves from becoming enmeshed in external or internal negativity. They offer advice on how to avoid intensifying existing negative situations, and to gradually turn them into positive ones.

I do not believe in "brushing under the rug" or ignoring the pain that many people are suffering.

If, in explaining the challenges and discussing my approach to dealing with them, some parts of my book seem overly "spiritual" or theological, out of touch with the reality of your particular circumstances, I ask your forgiveness in advance.

The information that I present here has proven to be very helpful to me and many others, and I offer it in the hopes that it will prove helpful to you as well.

I also hope and pray that the sympathy and compassion I feel toward those who are in very difficult and painful situations, whether in relationships, health, or finances, comes through in these pages as it does in real life, in my sessions.

Please trust that it is my sincere intention to help, not, G-d forbid, to hurt.

May the effort you are expending in reading these books and applying their advice be repaid by your quick and pleasant attainment of or return to health and happiness.

BeAhavas Yisrael,

Miriam Yerushalmi

To my children:

To my dearest son Yechezkal and to my dearest daughter, Chana Leah.

I pray that these words of our holy sages, found gathered together in this book help you reach greater heights.

My yearning to share these treasures with you – and with all of *Am Yisrael* I hope is captured and made manifest in this book. (Of course there is no replacement for the original sources.)

The information in this book has been the key to my heart and I so desire for you to have it too. Not a day has gone by since your births, without a prayer in my heart, that I wanted to be, for you, the best mother and a shining example of a true Jew.

Acknowledgements

This book is a combined effort of a team of knowledgeable, professional, skilled and talented individuals.

Avigail HaLevy and Chaya Sarah Cantor transcribed many of my classes, and helped edit them for use herein beautifully and creatively.

Rabbi Michael Seligson somehow always found time to help identify the many Chassidic sources for my lectures.

Rivka Zakutinski always helps me forge ahead. Her expertise and helping hand have given me the wherewithal to accomplish many of my goals.

Orah Baer Gerstl, whose encyclopedic knowledge enabled her to catch mistakes not only in the manuscript but in published texts that I cited, and who "fleshed out" the material, clarified the text, and provided footnotes.

Yaacov Dovid Shulman was invaluable in organizing and improving the flow of information, creating the bullet points, and transcribing the case studies.

Malka Schwartz gave insightful and constructive aid.

A very special thanks to Reva Baer, who pulled the pieces together and put the final polish on the manuscript.

Special thanks to Rabbi Shloma Majesky for his critique and advice as well as for giving permission to quote from his book *The Chassidic Approach to Joy.*

Special thanks to Rabbi Yonah Avtzon for giving permission to quote from *Sichos in English.*

Special thanks to Rabbi Yitzchak Ginsburgh for giving permission to quote from his book *The Mystery of Marriage.*

Special thanks to Rabbi Chaim Miller for his encouragement and for his assistance in getting this book published.

I am forever grateful to those *shluchim,* those messengers of Hashem and ambassadors of Judaism, who have impacted my life for the good, and there have been many. The Lubavitcher Rebbe, with his trademark *ahavas Yisrael,* his love for every Jew, was behind these individuals; teaching, inspiring, and driving them to give so much of themselves. He sent young couples to locations far and near to serve as leaders, guides, and role models for Jews who did not have the advantage of an authentic Jewish education and were unaware of many of the basic tenets and practices of their tradition. Almost all of the individuals I mention had been sent by the Rebbe on *shlichus.* (Presently, there are over 5,000 *shluchim* of the Lubavitcher Rebbe stationed all over the world to serve the needs of Jews and non-Jews in their locations... and the number continues to increase.)

I am particularly awed by the *shluchos* who, together with their husbands, and with modesty and utter selflessness, joyfully choose this life of *ahavas Yisrael* and dedication to their communities. They do so knowing that because of the remote locations in which they may live, they may have no choice but to send their young children away to board in the larger Jewish communities where proper Jewish schools exist (or, as may be more common now, homeschool them via online classrooms). Many of them regularly board jets in order to get to the nearest *mikvah* (ritual bath). The role models for these women were the Chabad Rebbetzins, and these righteous women have in turn become role models for us. I was fortunate to have met and been inspired by some of these "women of valor" in the course of my being invited to speak in their communities about marriage and other topics. I returned from each talk feeling encouraged and energized to continue my work in this world, with myself, my family, my clients, and my community.

When I was a child, I loved getting Shabbos candles at the Chabad booth at the Israel March, and the good feeling bridged over to Shabbos itself. The joy, hugs, and warmth at the Shabbos table of my Pre 1-A teacher, Mrs. Miriam Rabinowitz, inspired me to commit to *mitzvah* observance before my *Bat Mitzvah*.

Mr. and Mrs. Efrayim and Freida Bloom, my first *shluchim*, whose kindness in making me a member of the family built a bridge from their open home into my future—

for all those *mitzvos*, may both your souls be forever blessed and forever at peace. Chana Leah Weiner, (their daughter) and my best childhood friend—her love and acceptance literally saved my life and still does.

Rebbetzin Debbi Gordon of Encino, CA, was there for me at my next major milestone, when I married my husband David; although she had many demands on her time, as my *kallah* teacher she gave me her full attention each time we met—just as she had done when she was my high school teacher.

As we began and continued our journey through life together, my husband and I met many *shluchim*: Rabbi Meir and Rebbetzin Esther Gitlin of Thornhill, Ontario; Rabbi Itchel and Rebbetzin Pearl Krasniansky in Honolulu, Hawaii; Rabbi Avraham and Rebbetzin Yocheved Shemla in Maale Adumim, Israel; Levi and Sarah Volovik. Each of them in their own way welcomed us warmly and treated us like family. Their imprint remained, and to this day we consider them our extended family.

By 1999, when I met Rabbi Yosef and Rebbetzin Chanie Geisinsky (*shluchim* of Great Neck, NY), I had already been counseling individuals, couples, and families for 12 years. Based on my studies for a BA in Psychology and Child Development, and an MA in Psychology and Marriage and Family Counseling, I created and used customized meditations and guided imagery for my clients to help them achieve the positive thought patterns, emotional comfort, and behavioral changes necessary for inner peace and good relationships. Rabbi and Rebbetzin Geisinsky brought us to the life-giving wellsprings of Chabad Chassidus and guided us as we delved deeper into it. In turn I was able to incorporate Chassidic teachings of the Torah I learned into my counseling strategy and technique, frequently utilizing these concepts in creating new meditations and guided imagery. Without my Rav and *mashpia* (spiritual mentor), Rabbi Geisinsky, and my Rebbetzin, his wife Chanie, this book would not exist.

(Bear with me readers, as I take this golden opportunity to really thank everyone for all their years (if not) decades of help.)

All these people, as well as others, whom I may have inadvertently omitted, from around the world who greatly assisted me in becoming who I am today. They enabled me to share selected teachings of Torah and Chassidus, presented and applied in a manner which serves as a prescription and roadmap to self actualization. So here goes!

I give credit to the students in my weekly Chassidus classes in Great Neck and Borough Park, as well as in the 770 synagogue under the aegis of the *Beis Medrash Lenashim Ubanos* organization in Crown Heights, who for over almost two decades now have required me continually to reach for and achieve more meticulous precision and depth in my understanding of Chassidus and its applications.

Thanks to Ariella Benchayion, coordinator of *Beis Medrash Lenashim Ubnos*, 770. As well as, thanks to *N'shei Chabad*, who were the first to ask me to speak publicly at local events: Shterna Spritzer, President of *N'shei Chabad*; Chana Morosov, coordinator of *N'shei* events and events outside our community, Rochie Serebranski, and Nisi Streicher, head of *Ahavas Chesed* women's learning in Borough Park and on *Kol Haloshon*, who has also published my work in *B'simcha* Magazine.

Special thanks to all my very dear fiends, my soul sisters, who have been like my extended family and not only have been very supportive of me, but also have helped my non-profit organization called SANE.

Faye Doomchin, Nushien Lavi, Jenia Yashaya, Joan Goodman, Eden Cooper, Edna Guilor, Perla Cegla, Monica Alon, Mahdokht Sherian, Esther Abeniem; Kaila Feldman, Nechama Dina Gitter; Aliza Elkayam; Nechama Dina Zweibel; Devorie Botnick, Mariasha Dejon and family; Bailey Levy and family; Shulamit Kaye, Sara Neman, Leah Malekanes, Simcha Cohen, Daniella Lazell, Tova Bronshtein, and Elana Butler,

Special thanks to Jennifer Schuller, who volunteers to review and edit my work, Yael Dorn, whose reviewed my work and whose idea it was to make Meditations cards.

Special thanks to Shoshana Bander; who arranges my speaking engagements for Shabbatons.

Special thanks to Malka Schwartz who hosted my *shiurim* in her home and arranged for others to do so both locally and abroad, and for years assisted me with her editing expertise. And to Rivka Rothchild who first hosted classes by her home. And to Ferrie Sedaghchour, Orely Yagoubian and Roya Yagoubian for years hosting classes by their homes.

Special thanks to Margerie Libbin helped edit my work and volunteers her time as a counselor for SANE.

Special thanks to Chana Kaiman, my colleague, who connected me to *Jewish Press*, *Nefesh* international, hosted and arranged classes, critiqued, edited, volunteers her time as a counselor for SANE and did the leg work for the publication of this book.

Special thanks to Dr Carol Lerman, a dear friend, who has given funds for SANE over the years and shares her home for class events.

Special thanks to Cindy Gold hosted monthly *Rosh Chodesh* classes by her.

Special thanks to Leah Ben Mor (Laurie Cohen), in addition to transcribing lessons, for years volunteered her time organizing speaking engagements across America.

Special thanks to Leah Kustiner, Nomi Bhatia, and Dalia Rivka BenElyahoo volunteered their time to help arrange my classes that are now available through Free Conference call and Torahanytime.com.

Special thanks to, Sara Esther Speilman, whose writing skills helped edit so many of my projects.

Special thanks to Dr. and Mrs. Trappler opened doors for us when we first arrived in New York who eagerly assisted and guided me with many projects.

A very special thanks to Devora Kozlik for your friendship, for your selfless dedication on behalf of *Sparks* and for being my supportive supervisor over the years.

A very special thanks to Esther Kenigsberg, founder of *Sparks*, for your selfless dedication to women and their families, who not only has become a dear friend, but who has had unwavering faith in my work, posting classes and many of my mindful meditation on her audio library, posting my articles in her magazine True Balance, introduced me to Dr Abraham Twerski and providing me with continuos training in the field of mental health, most particularly for PPD through her sponsored training workshops.

To my dear friend, Devorah Hakimian, who deserves special thanks. She has supported my work continuously for over seventeen years by volunteering her time and her talents. Without her, I don't know where my organization SANE would be today.

Of course, my dear extended family: Ricky Horowitz was like a second mom; her husband Al; Ami Horowitz and family; Rachel Sokolovski and Uncle Phima; Cousin Miriam Sokolovski; Aunt Zahava and uncle Sal, Cousin Edna and husband Morris; Cousin Poriah; Cousin Serena Karten and family; Lila Beychok Boyer and family; Dan Beychok and family.

And particularly, my dear real soul sisters: Ruth Himmelman and Chana Levy, and their families.

To my dear parents, Esther Levy and Gabriel Levy, for their *mesiras nefesh* to ensure I had a Jewish education and always being there for me.

To my dear children Yechezkal Moshe and Chana Leah, thank you for being you. Thank you for your love and friendship and being my wonderful partners, for being the ultimate catalysts for my personal development. Your presence in my life has motivated me to search for the deepest truths, with the goal of becoming the best that I can be.

To my dear husband, the other half of my soul, David Yerushalmi—to paraphrase Rabbi Akiva, "Everything that is mine, is his." He has always believed in me and always supported me in all my projects, in every way: financially, emotionally, and way more actually. In fact, he works tirelessly on behalf of the Jewish people and is a true

Maccabee of this generation. May Hashem bless you in everything.

To the Lubavitcher Rebbe, Rabbi Menachem Mendel Schneerson, and all our Rebbes, for all their *mesiras nefesh* (self-sacrifice) and life's work.

Ultimately, I owe my thanks to Hashem for His care and His kindness, for leading me to Torah and opening my heart to the inner dimensions of Chassidus.

For all your help, may Hashem bless each and everyone of you and your families forever !!!

Forever grateful,

Miriam Yerushalmi

Chana's Leah's Song Dedicated to Her Grandma

Legacy.

Tears have been wept down from my eyes
Bubby, Bubby, where are you now?
I can see your holy face, your image in my mind
Come back to me to those Shabbos nights

She worked and toiled to fulfill her goal

Let heaven and above bless her soul

A true mother and eishes chayil

That was what she portrayed

Self-sacrifice is what she clearly made

The woman who fought for what was right

A full-time nurse way into the night

She is loving, she is caring; to this very day

Bubby, you always remain in my heart

The thoughtful lessons which you pointed out

I will carry your legacy on!

We will carry your legacy on!

With sincere appreciation to all those who donated towards the publication of this book.

Tova Bronshtein, in loving memory of
her mother, Miriam bas Chana

Malka Rivka Gerardino, in loving memory
of her mother, Sara bas Floria Maraia.

Simcha and Tamar Adelstein, in honor of the marriage
of their daughter Chaya to Nathaniel Levy

Shulamit and Baruch Kaye, as a *zechus* for their children
Sara Chaya Bracha, Avraham Mordechai, Shira Batya,
Aryeh Chaim Dovid, Yosef Ovadia, and Simcha Meira, and
in loving memory of their dear father and father-in-law,

לע"נ הרב עובדיה בן חיים דוד רוזנברג

May it give him much *nachas* that the teachings of *Chassidus*
found in this book have increased *shalom bayis* in the world.

Rivka Bat Daisy

Zalman Nissan ben Baruch

Ahron Meir ben Baruch

My dear Grandmother, Esther (Levy) bas Miriam

My Uncle Shmuel (Levy) ben Benieyahu

My Aunt Sarah bas Benieyahu
Ashraf Yaffa bat Rabbi Mola Menashe

In loving memory of my dear father-in law, Yisrael Avraham ben Moshe

In memory of my dear mother-in-law, Leah bas Avraham

In memory of Sorah Feiga bas Moshe

Inspiration From Rabbi Gabi And Rivkah Holtzberg H"YD

For over eight years, the manuscript for this book sat in raw form in my computer. I always thought I would publish this book eventually, but given the reality of my hectic life as the working mother of young children, many of my projects were relegated to the back burner. Yet hearing stories of Gabi and Rivki Holtzberg at a memorial service touched me so deeply, that I resolved then and there to begin preparing my manuscripts for publication as a way of honoring their memories. As my situation had not changed much, the process was far from instantaneous. With G-d's help, however, the book finally came to fruition.

A memorial service for Rabbi Gabi and Rivki Holtzberg was held in a synagogue in Great Neck, NY. The news of their murder had been devastating. The emotion in the air was palpable. Two beautiful young souls who had dedicated themselves to helping others had been snatched away so brutally. The tragic loss was felt by Jews and non-Jews all over the world.

The memorial event was surreal for me; I was in such pain yet at the same time felt so proud and inspired by the Holtzbergs. I felt as though I was a witness to the self-sacrifice of the Maccabees, Queen Esther, or—perhaps most appropriately—Rabbi Akiva, who sanctified G-d's name as he was tortured to death for teaching Torah.

In my mind's eye I visualized this holy couple as if they were still in Mumbai, in their first tiny apartment, where Rivkah Holtzberg prepared food on the floor because she had no kitchen counters and guests enjoyed their meals sitting around a bed because they did not have a table. Gabi and Rivki were the epitome of kindness.

One man at the memorial service, who was fortunate to have met Rabbi Holtzberg, recounted that on several occasions when as was his norm he showed up at the Mumbai marketplace at six in the morning, Rabbi Holtzberg was also there, surrounded by bags of food. It became clear to him that Rabbi Holtzberg was not in the marketplace to do business, so out of curiosity he finally approached Gabi to ask him why he was there. Rabbi Holtzberg answered that he wanted to ensure that any Jew doing business in the marketplace would have easy access to kosher food.

The man marveled that Rabbi Holtzberg assumed this kindness personally, rather than delegate it to someone else. After all, Rabbi Holtzberg was a brilliant and learned man, a *sofer* (scribe), a *mohel* (one who performs circumcisions), a *shochet* (ritual slaughterer), who had many other obligations. He was a visionary, who could have devoted his time to "higher" pursuits. Yet, he spent many of his early mornings looking after the mundane needs of his fellow Jews.

Another man, who frequently did business in Mumbai, told of the mysterious package he was presented with by the clerk when he checked into his hotel late on a Friday afternoon. When the businessman asked who it was from he was surprised by the answer, "It's from your friend," because as far as he knew, he had no friends in Mumbai. He opened the package to find a hot gourmet Shabbos meal along with a note from Rabbi Holtzberg welcoming him to Mumbai. The businessman called the rabbi to thank him, and they arranged to meet at the shul the next day. This kindness was the beginning of a special relationship with the Holtzbergs which grew over the years.

It was told that during the *shiva* (mourning period), a woman approached Rivki's mother and handed her a package, saying: "This belonged to your daughter." The woman explained that while in Mumbai, she had gotten into some legal trouble and had approached Rivki for advice. Rivki gave the woman her own Shabbos dress and diamond engagement ring so that the woman would look respectable when facing the authorities. With Rivki's backing, the woman was able to convince the court that she was a law-abiding person, and she now wanted to return the items that Rivki had lent her.

The Holtzbergs were undeniably great people. They were a couple dedicated to serving Hashem, who radiated love and acted with kindness to all. In his last Shabbos speech before he and his wife were tragically murdered, Rabbi Holtzberg even spoke about kindness to animals!

It would be a mistake to assume that Gabi and Rivki's greatness lay solely in their dedication and kindness to others. After their passing, many spoke of the evident *shalom bayis* and the special relationship they shared with each other. Sandra Samuel, their dedicated nanny and helper who saw how the Holtzbergs related to each other on a daily basis in their home, said of Rivki, "I don't think that she could imagine life without that man." The Torah teaches that the highest level of relationship husband and wife can reach is that at which they cannot envision life without the other. This special couple seemed to have already reached this level despite their being married for only a relatively short time.

The positive relationship between husband and wife is worthy in and of itself, as it brings the holy *Shechinah*, G-d's Presence, into the world. However, it can be even more than that. It can be a great inspiration to others. People look at a couple with a good relationship and say to themselves, "I want that." That desire can even inspire them to take on an entire life of Torah and mitzvos.

May we all take upon ourselves a commitment to demonstrate greater kindness and selflessness when it comes to dealing with others, beginning with our own spouses. Let us try to increase our efforts to help our fellow Jews, using whatever talents G-d has given us—as Gabi and Rivki Holtzberg exemplified.

1

—

Marriage As An Expression of G-d's Kindness

Marital harmony, *shalom bayis*, is not something that a couple attains automatically by virtue of being married. Were that the case, there would be no *mitzvos* associated with its achievement. It would be easy, but empty. Rather, *shalom bayis* is a goal for which to strive, and the effort is part of the reward.

Married people—or single people observing married couples—may often wonder at the apparently unnecessary difficulties marriage presents. Why should men and women have been created to be so different from each other? Wouldn't it have made marriage, and life, so much easier if a couple's outlooks, perceptions, and temperaments were naturally more in sync? Yet, G-d designed marriage to present challenges.

G-d's kindness is evident in all His creations. While someone in an unhappy relationship may not recognize the kindness that is inherent in the marriage bond, it is in reality a G-dly path to finding one's *shleimus*, completion.

Husband and Wife: One Soul, Two Expressions

The verse in Proverbs (18:22) says, "*Motza ishah, motza tov*, he who has found a wife has found good." That is, marriage is beneficial to a man. Why would the word "found" be written twice? According to the *Zohar*, a husband and wife are one entity that has been separated into two. They are incomplete without each other.

A little background is necessary here. The human soul actually comprises five levels. The first three, *nefesh* (spirit), *ruach* (breath), and *neshama* (soul), pertain to our everyday lives. *Nefesh* refers to biological life, *ruach* to emotional life, and *neshama* to intellectual life. The other two levels, *chaya* (living) and *yechida* (essence), transcend the range of the physical and affect us from above.[1]

Up in heaven, a husband and wife are one entity contained within one soul. G-d separates this unified entity into two before sending them to earth. When a couple dates, Hashem gives each soul mate an extra connection to the power of their transcendent soul, at the *chaya* level, so that they will be able to draw wisdom from this higher level of spirituality in order to help them recognize that they are soul mates. Experiencing the connection to their *chaya* level of their soul allows them to see the good in each other.

Mutual Kindness

At the same time, each partner in the relationship is also equipped with temporary blinders, as it were, to prevent them from seeing the negative too soon. Hashem wants them to recognize the positive aspects first. Once they marry, however, G-d returns the *chaya* dimension of their soul to the transcendent sphere, and without the active assistance of the *chaya* pointing out the good, each partner tends to see certain aspects of the other's character that were hidden before.

That is why the verse says "*motza*, find" twice. Now the couple needs to find the good in each other on their own, so

1   Cf. Rabbi Simon Jacobson, *60 Days: A Spiritual Guide to the High Holidays* (New York: Kiyum Press, 2003).

to speak. But how can they do this? As each partner refines themselves by taking steps to diminish negative traits—anger, lust, sadness—that *chaya* dimension of their souls has more space to return.

When this positivity is strengthened, the entire relationship is invigorated. Once merged, the reunited soul will not only reach the level at which the two halves were together in heaven, but surpass it. This is indicated by the fact that in heaven the two halves of the soul are back to back, but when they are reunited here below, they are face to face and heart to heart. The repetition of the word "found" reflects this double benefit as well as a couple's double bond: at first when they are united in heaven, and again when they find each other—and the good in each other—in this world.

As the Rebbe writes[2]:

A husband and wife are not two separate entities, but are one. And, as in the case of physical body, when any part is strengthened and invigorated, it automatically adds vigor and strength to all the other parts, so, and much more so, is the case with husband and wife who have been married C'das Moshe V'Yisrael [according to the Torah of Moses and Israel], "the benefit to one is a benefit to both."

A young couple inevitably experiences certain difficulties, trials, and sometimes even crises, chas veshalom [heaven forbid]. But when one realizes that these are only trials designed to

---

2   Rabbi Yosef Yitzchak Schneerson, *Letters from the Rebbe*. (New York: Otsar Sifrei Lubavitch, Inc., 1997).

strengthen the foundations of the home, which is to be an
everlasting edifice (binyan adei ad), and as the Torah states, "For
God tries you to make known your love," etc. (Deuteronomy
13:4), one appreciates them in their true perspective. For,
in sending these difficulties and trials, God also provides the
capacity to overcome them. Far from being discouraged by such
difficulties, one considers them as challenges to be overcome, in
order to reap the benefits that are inherent in them.

Producing Peace

What is the kindness behind the original separation of the
soul? The Rebbe explained that *shalom*, peace, is not the
mere absence of opposition. True peace is something that
is created after a period of opposition. Reminiscent of the
creation of the world, in the creation of a happy home there
must be some chaos out of which peaceful order is formed.

As the Rebbe writes[3]:

If truth be told, the core aspect of peace only exists where
there was previously opposition and division.

The concept of "peace" implies that there exist two forces
that by their very nature oppose and clash with each other. It
is the quality of "peace" that brings them together. However,
between two things that never were in opposition we cannot say

3   Rabbi Shneur Zalman of Liadi, *Lessons in Tanya*, transcribed by Rabbi Yosef
     Karasik; translated by Rabbi Yosef Wineberg and Rabbi Sholom B. Wineberg.
     (New York: Kehot Publication Society, 1998).

that "peace" was ever achieved between them, when in point of fact they never warred with each other.

The chaos of the opposing natures of men and women was carefully designed to be, ultimately, beneficial. Men and women were created to be different in order that they would use their differences to achieve the common goal of a unified, harmonic home and family.

This is made very clear in the Biblical story of the Patriarch Yitzchak (Isaac) and his wife, the Matriarch Rivkah (Rebekah), who were blessed with children only after Yitzchak prayed "opposite his wife" (Genesis 25:21).

Yitzchak appears in the Torah as a quiet person, accepting his life's events without outward questions. As Rabbi DovBer Pinson explains[4]:

"The masculine energy in the universe is a forward outward movement, which can manifest as assertiveness, extraversion and contribution. The feminine energy is manifested as inward movement, acceptance and receiving. It is important to note that men and women alike contain both masculine and feminine energy in varying degrees....

Yitzchak ... was, in effect, existing in a place of femininity, as the AriZal teaches. [Rivkah] was completely representative of femininity and therefore they were unable to create something new together.

---

4   Rabbi DovBer Pinson, http://iyyun.com/teachings/energy/energy-of-the-week-parshas-toldos. Published March 14, 2011.

In order to create a new existence, opposing forces need to come together. The antithesis creates the possibility of a synthesis and a new direction. From the tension and eventual fusion between opposites, a third reality, or a new life, emerges."

The relationship of Yitzchak and Rivkah could be fruitful only when both spouses expressed their unique, gender-based opposite natures. It was only when Yitzchak, manifesting his natural masculine character, finally stood and prayed "opposite" Rivkah, the personification of femininity, each beseeching G-d in their own distinctive voice yet in unison, that they were able to create new life together.

Disagreement Is Not Disaster

How does all this relate to *your* relationship? It shows that differences between spouses are not only normal but are purposely designed by G-d. A certain level of misunderstanding and disagreement are to be expected in any relationship. Realize that you are not the only couple on the block whose opinions conflict with each other at times. Feeling unhappy or disappointed with your spouse, or feeling as though you two disagree on everything, does not necessarily mean that you married the wrong person. Even the conviction that you and your spouse argue more than the average couple, does not indicate that you were not meant to be a couple. (It does show, though, that you are doing the right thing by seeking help to change the way you relate to one another.)

Selfish vs. Selfless

Nowadays, many marriages suffer from the distorted notion of love held by one spouse, or by both spouses. The secular view of love and marriage which has crept into our society's consciousness is vastly different from the Torah view of marriage and love.

The secular view of love stresses "romance." But romantic love is essentially about gratifying one's ego, and the underlying idea is actually selfishness. Unless a person's imagination is trained to see beyond its selfish desires, it will become fixated on fulfilling them above all else. The focus in modern secular society leans heavily toward sensory and sensual stimulation, and away from spiritual introspection.

The Torah view of love, though, is based on selflessness.[5] The hallmarks of a Torah-true relationship are common goals, genuine caring, and sensitivity towards and respect for the other. Rabbi Yitzchak Ginsburgh describes the difference between the two views as "unrectified" versus "rectified" love: "unrectified love is focused on oneself; one may think he's loving someone else, but he's really only

5   Rabbi Yitzchak Ginsburgh, *The Mystery of Marriage* (Kfar Chabad: Gal Einai, 1999), page 52.

loving himself. Rectified love involves learning how to focus one's love and concern on someone else."[6]

Listen to the Right Voice

Each of us possesses two inner voices, the *yetzer hatov* ("good inclination") and the *yetzer hara* ("evil inclination"). The *yetzer hara* is programmed to bombard us with a never-ending stream of negative thoughts in order to undermine our desire to do good deeds and do what is good for us.

In the context of a troubled relationship, the *yetzer hara* may manifest itself as a constant inner monologue whispering that your spouse is inappropriate for or unworthy of you. Your *yetzer hara* may have you worried that your partner is influencing you in a negative way and bringing out the worst in you. It may encourage you to believe the erroneous idea that if you do not feel passionately "in love" at most moments of the day, then your marriage is empty.

The *yetzer hara* may confuse you so that you cannot properly cope with the situation. It may lead you to consider drastic and even tragic steps. It may have you convinced that once released from this relationship you would be able to move on into a better life.

Often, a person who is doing his or her best will feel dragged down by their spouse, particularly if their partner

6   Ibid., p. 71.

is not acting in a loving manner. Then the partner's every word can be perceived as criticism—whether mild or harsh, intentional or inadvertent—and every facial expression can be seen as one of disappointment or disgust. This situation can wear a person down into believing that he or she is a failure, and lead to berating oneself for not being able to deal with the situation. Afflicted with doubts about one's relationship and self-worth, the mitzvah of *shalom bayis* may become overwhelming. Subsequently, one's other mitzvah obligations may also appear too difficult to handle, until finally one may feel that life as a whole is a burden.

Destined to Be Together

The Lubavitcher Rebbe teaches that husband and wife should believe that they are destined to be together, as if there were no other human beings on earth, as was the case with Adam and Chavah (Eve). Adam and Chavah both knew that they were destined to be together and did not consider the possibility that they had married the wrong person— since there was, after all, no one else to choose from.

If Adam and Chavah had lived today, it is likely that they would have gotten divorced.[7] Many a modern-day marriage counselor would have encouraged Adam to leave a wife who had done wrong and persuaded him to do wrong as well—and to do it quickly, before the situation became

---

7   Rabbi Moshe Bogomilsky, *Vedibarta Bam: Rosh Hashana, Yom Kippur, and Sukkot* (New York: Merkos Linyonei Chinuch, 2006) p. 21.

complicated by the arrival of children. But Adam did not divorce his wife and in fact remained married to her for many hundreds of years afterward. What helped make this possible?

The answer may be found in the verse that appears immediately after Adam and Chavah are punished for their sin (Genesis 4:1): "The man had known his wife, Chavah, and she conceived and bore Cain." One of the meanings of *had known* is "understood." After the sin of eating from the Tree of Knowledge, Adam gained insight into Chavah's behavior. He understood that she was only human and that as such she could err. Because he had this realization, he did not blame her, abuse her, and divorce her, but remained with her, and together they brought children into this world.

Prayer Stages of Marriage

Rabbi Yoseph Geisinsky[8] understands the patriarch's marriages in comparison to the prayer service each one instituted, and applies this understanding to contemporary culture. Avraham (Abraham) instituted *Shacharit*, the morning prayer; Yitzchak instituted the afternoon prayer, *Minchah*; and Yaakov (Jacob) instituted the evening prayer, *Maariv*. Our marital relationships similarly have a morning, afternoon, and evening stage.

8   Rabbi Yoseph Geisinsky, "Three Components of Marriage" weekly email, Oct. 24, 2013.

The morning *Shacharit* stage comes when we meet our soul mate. The hope for our future together is exciting and inspirational. The special moonlight moments of romance and passion, of discovering unexpected depths in our spouse, is the *Maariv* of marriage. But the main stage is that of *Minchah*, the simple, non-dramatic commitment to each other through the difficult times as well as the loving times. The *Minchah* stage can never be experienced before marriage. For that reason, the Torah tells us that only after marriage does Yitzchak come to love Rivkah. And the longer they were married, the more he loved her.

That the first Jewish courtship and marriage described thoroughly in the Torah is the one of Yitzchak and Rivkah[9] teaches us a fundamental principle: enduring love does not happen as a result of passion and romance, which can easily fade away, but rather as a result of an appreciation of the inner qualities and values of the other person.

As Rabbi Geisinsky says, "Our culture knows how to pray *Shacharit* and *Maariv*. We need to discover the secret of *Minchah*."

---

9   This is not to say that Avraham and Sarah did not have a loving relationship, but the feelings between them at the time of their marriage are not explicitly recorded. It is noteworthy here that the circumstances surrounding the marriages of couples mentioned in the Torah prior to Yitzchak and Rivkah were not described beyond, for example (Gen. 11:29), "and Avram and Nahor took for themselves wives."

Greet the Challenge

Let us recognize—or rediscover—and appreciate the good qualities in ourselves and in our spouses. Furthermore, let us work on changing our negative traits into positive ones. Now is the time to delve into the inner work that will help you keep the love within your marriage alive and your relationship healthy.

I won't tell you that this process will be easy. Intimate relationships can be inherently challenging, and the process of improving the way you relate to your spouse may be fraught with difficulty. Progress is not linear. One day you may feel as if you are soaring toward perfection in your relationship; the next day, you may feel that you are backsliding far and fast. But strengthening your marriage is a goal that is well worth the struggle.

Exercises/Meditations

Note: I have found that visualization (also called guided imagery) is a potent tool for personal growth. We each possess an almost limitless ability to train our brain to get in the habit of positive responses. As with any other muscle, exercising your brain increases its capacity over time; the more you use imagery the more your brain comes accustomed to it. Skill at using imagery increases with practice, so don't worry if your first attempts don't seem effective. Some people are naturally adept at imagery while others need time to get the hang of it. Persevere, and eventually you will be able to incorporate into your daily routine the behavioral changes that you are targeting. [Please see Appendix for more information on guided imagery.]

Visualization is quite simple. It can be done anywhere, although it is best done in quiet surroundings where you are not likely to be interrupted. Sit upright, as that position is most conducive to clear thinking. The chair should be supportive and allow your feet to touch the floor. Sitting in a recliner may help you to relax, but avoid overstuffed ones and do not recline so far that you relax to the point of falling asleep. Close your eyes, take a deep breath or two, and try to clear both your mind and your muscles of tension as much as possible. At first you may feel even more stressed at the thought of "forcing" yourself to relax, but this will be overcome with time and practice.

Then, orchestrate a video in your head of specific scenarios in your life. Picture yourself modeling the behavior you desire to achieve. For example, visualize a scenario in which you respond to your spouse in a calm and loving manner. Mentally rehearsing again and again the successful outcome that you want to achieve in your life will have a profound impact on your attitudes and reactions. The sustained concentration you gain from these exercises will improve your abilities in all areas.

During your visualizations, you may examine your relationship with your spouse, perhaps utilizing the following suggestions.

Visualize your soul within you. See it as one half of a whole. Visualize your soul as seeking completion. Then look at or visualize your spouse, but see beyond the physical: visualize the other part of your soul within your spouse. Finally, visualize the two halves uniting.

Consider the differences between you and your spouse. Reframe in a positive way any negative view you may have of these differences. If one of you is serious while the other is lighthearted, rather than say, "He/She never takes anything seriously!" or "He/She just has no sense of humor!" say, "Isn't it great that he/she can see the humor in this situation?" or, "My spouse always treats every situation with respect."

Commend yourself for having taken the first step toward improving your marriage.

Points for Practical Reflection

- The Torah views marriage as leading to love, as opposed to the secular view that love leads to marriage.

- The different temperaments of husband and wife demonstrate the limitless aspect of their one soul.

- Like Adam and Chavah, you and your spouse were chosen by Hashem to be partners.

- Every husband and wife, like Yitzchak and Rivkah, have different strengths to contribute to a marriage. These strengths are meant to complement each other and all are necessary to achieve your shared goal of building a successful, happy Torah home.

- The challenges of your relationship were designed by G-d specifically to strengthen your marriage.

- Feeling unhappy or disappointed with your spouse does not mean that you married the wrong person.

- Tension in your marriage is a cue that you can work to reveal your love for yourself, your spouse, and Hashem.

2
—

Put Your Imagination To Work For Your Marriage

The paramount goal in marriage should be to achieve that level of unity at which a couple has become a single entity on earth, just as they were in heaven. When we work hard to achieve this level of unity, G-d rewards us by enabling us to achieve the personal transformation to which we aspire.

In this regard, the Lubavitcher Rebbe writes[10]:

A Jewish marriage is called a binyan adei ad, "an everlasting edifice." This means that the Jewish home and married life must be built and structured on the foundations

10 Schneerson, *Letters from the Rebbe* vol. 4, page 151.

of Torah and mitzvos, as emphasized by our sages, whose saintliness was matched by their true wisdom.

The metaphor is meaningful in that when it comes to laying the foundation of a building, it is of no concern what neighbors or passers-by might think of the outer attractiveness of the foundation, much less what scoffers might say about it. What is important is that the foundation be tested and consist of durable material that can be tested to ascertain that it can withstand any erosive elements and that it be strong enough to support the upper floors that will be added to it.

When you build your marriage on the foundations of Torah and *mitzvos*—which is no small task, for it requires you to refine your actions, thoughts and speech—it is as though you have built your own personal *Bais HaMikdash*.

In his letters to people undergoing marital difficulties, the Lubavitcher Rebbe stressed the greatness of *shalom bayis* and the necessity of doing everything possible to improve the relationship, especially when children are involved:

"You got married in accordance with Torah. The marital blessings were made with Hashem's holy Name. You both were blessed with children, the greatest blessing a couple can have. Together with this, you both were given a great mitzvah, raising and educating your children, culminating with bringing them to the chuppah. All these rich opportunities were given to both of you as a complete whole unit. ... Understandably, you and your husband can share your issues with a rav and ask him to be a mediator.... Both of you need to pull together and improve the shalom bayis. If you truly want to keep the family together,

you will surely be successful. The merit of your children that you brought into the world will help you accomplish your goal."[11]

The Rebbe emphasized that, as the Talmud says (*Makos* 10b) "in the way a person wishes to go, he will be led" with Heavenly assistance.

Improve the Foundation

Rather than giving up on a relationship, focus your attention and emotional energy on improving it. This involves intensive work on oneself. The process of growing from being an individual with his or her own agenda, into a couple pursuing a common aim, requires thinking outside of oneself, in order to develop sensitivity and respect for the partner. The "unrectified" perception from which many suffer can be corrected by incorporating these qualities of care and concern more fully into one's character.

Once the foundation is healthy, a loving, Torah-true relationship can be built. It may take some time to see results, but ultimately your efforts will be rewarded.

There was once a woman who, as she took stock of the resolutions she had made a year ago, felt discouraged. She saw that despite her hard work, she still had the same flaws that she had had then. She felt that her efforts had been in vain, and she wanted to give up altogether.

11   Rabbi Chaim Dalfin, *The Rebbe's Advice* (New York: Mendelsohn, 1997).

As a last-ditch effort, she went to talk to her Rebbetzin.

The Rebbetzin sighed and asked, "Do you know how long it takes for a bamboo tree to grow as tall as a building?"

The woman looked at her with a puzzled expression on her face and said, "No, I have no idea."

The Rebbetzin answered the question herself. "After the farmer plants the seed in the ground, he waters and fertilizes it. Only after five years of cultivating the bamboo plant does he begin to see some growth. But in the fifth year, the bamboo grows ninety feet in a matter of only six weeks!" With a warm smile, the Rebbetzin asked: "So now can you answer my question? How long does it take the bamboo tree to grow so high?"

The woman confidently answered: "Six weeks."

The Rebbetzin leaned forward, looked the other woman in the eye, and said gently: "That is your mistake. It takes five years *and* six weeks. If the farmer would have stopped cultivating the bamboo at any point during those five years, the plant would have died." She continued, "What was happening during all those years? Underneath the ground an enormous network of roots was developing to support the bamboo's sudden growth. Growth takes patience and perseverance. Every step you take makes an impact. You may not see changes right away, but change is happening. With commitment and determination to achieve your goals, and of course with G-d's help, you too will eventually reach great heights."

Be Realistic

In this era of instant technology and labor-saving devices, it is easy to lose patience both with ourselves and with others. We have become so accustomed to immediate gratification that we get frustrated when we fail to see instant improvement in either our own character or in that of our family members, including our spouse.

Setting unrealistic goals for yourself and then failing to achieve them leads to feeling stressed, inadequate, and angry. When you place such undue pressure on yourself, you create an internal dynamic that can lead you to lose control over your emotions. Feeling angry at yourself leads you to feel less loving and patient—if not downright hostile—toward others. Often your closest family members will suffer the brunt of your inner distress.

The emotional fallout can also lead to physical distress. The symptoms associated with this include weight gain, mood swings, fatigue, and a diminished interest in intimacy. In general, both men and women can be afflicted with these and other physical symptoms of stress.

The Alter Rebbe taught that just as a sick person will do whatever is necessary to heal himself, so too a person who is not well emotionally or has some improper character trait ought to do whatever it takes to heal or improve himself (*Tanya, Iggeres Ha-Teshuvah* chap. 3, p. 93; chap. 10, page 230). Similarly, if your spouse is ailing emotionally, you will do well to invest time in helping heal him or her, even if that means taking time within the day away from others in your family and other responsibilities. Such actions will ultimately benefit the entire family.

Improving your character is not a goal that you can accomplish overnight. Rather, it is a lifelong process. Just as you would not expect an infant to run a marathon, so too you cannot expect to transform yourself in one leap into a paragon of virtue and a perfect spouse. Progress is best made through small, incremental steps.

Tools for Change

Fortunately, the Torah provides us with tools we can use to respond to the relentless demands of daily life without losing our composure or dignity. In particular, the Torah teaches us to have *bitachon*: trust that Hashem is good and does good.

As you take your first step toward transformation, you may have absolute faith that with G-d's help you will achieve your goal. As our Sages teach (*Shabbos* 104a), "A person who comes to purify himself is helped from above." In this vein, *Chassidus* homiletically interprets the verse in *Pirkei Avos* (Ethics of the Fathers 2:1), "Know what is above you" to mean: "Know that what is above is *from* you." The way we behave on earth has an impact on what happens in Heaven. If we behave as we should, we draw the good from Above into our lives.

In *Likkutei Dibburim,* the *Frierdiker* ("Previous") *Rebbe,* Rabbi Yosef Yitzchak Schneersohn (the sixth Lubavitcher Rebbe, also known as "the Rebbe Rayatz," 1880-1950) comments on the verse in *Tehillim* (Psalms 55:23), "Cast your burden upon Hashem and He will sustain you," that we should turn to Hashem not only for our material needs but for our spiritual needs as well. When we set out to refine ourselves and ask Hashem to help us, He gives us the tools with which to do so. Thus, the Hebrew word for "tool" or "vessel," *kli,* is related to the words *kalkalah,* "sustain" and *kol,* "everything."

Hashem provides us with the wherewithal—such as wisdom, energy and opportunity—to elevate our souls.

Prayer is Potent

The Alter Rebbe tells us in *Tanya* that during Rosh Hashanah when the shofar is blown, a new level of *moychin,* intellectual capacity, is being drawn down into the world. At that time we have a particular ability and opportunity to reach that new level. But we actually have access to this new energy every day when we pray. During the time of prayer, we are able to unite the three levels of knowledge: *Chochmah, Binah* and *Da'as.*[12]

---

12 *Tanya, Iggeres Hakodesh* chap. 14 (page 240); Please see Appendix for an explanation of the three levels.

It may be difficult to summon up the concentration necessary to grasp this energy, but as with any other endeavor, the result is worth the effort.

The Rebbe Rashab (Rabbi Sholom DovBer Schneersohn, the fifth Lubavitcher Rebbe, 1866-1920) taught that the more you "crush" your will by *daven*ing (praying) even when you don't feel like doing so, the less you will be "crushed" by life's events[13]: "The crushing does not necessarily need to come from on high, G-d forbid; it suffices that a person demeans and humbles himself. Regarding this, the Sages remark, 'only with a sense of earnestness may one begin to pray,' referring to the quality of surrender and humility. It is precisely in this way that a person will reach a more transcendent, sublime level through his prayer."

The strength you develop to fight your *yetzer hara* during prayer will stand by you at all other times.

Prayer is a very potent and reliable means by which to subdue and direct our animal soul. It should be appreciated as a multi-faceted tool as well, for in addition to bringing us closer to G-d, prayer is a tremendous aid in self-improvement. Prayer has a greater influence on our emotions than even Torah study does. Torah study affects one's ability to understand the greatness of G-d, but as the Rebbe Rashab teaches, "refinement and purification of one's

13   Rabbi Shalom Dov Ber Schneersohn, *The Power of Return* (New York: Kehot Publication Society, 2005) p. 38.

natural emotions is achieved only through the service of prayer. Not through Torah study."[14]

Unblemished Sacrifices

Prayer today takes the place of offering sacrifices in the Bais Hamikdash. When you *daven*, it is as though you are bringing a sacrifice, which must be unblemished. Negativity in your heart is like a blemish which must be healed in order for your prayers to be acceptable. The *Tzemach Tzedek* (Rabbi Menachem Mendel Schneersohn, the third Rebbe, 1789 – 1866) taught that since the soul of every Jew is connected to all other Jews, if you harbor hatred towards yourself or towards someone else, your heart is not whole.[15]

This incompleteness will make it difficult for your prayers to be answered, as if the gate into the prayer hall is locked and your key is broken. Do not be discouraged from praying, though, even if traces of ill-will still linger within your soul. *Ahavas Yisrael*, love for your fellow Jew, is a key that will open the gate to G-d's mercy. The more you develop this love, the more you strengthen your ability to connect to G-d.

---

14   Rabbi Sholom Dov Ber Schneerson, *Kuntres HaTefillah* (New York: Kehot Publication Society, 1992), p. 45. For more details, please refer to my book *Reaching New Heights Through Prayer and Meditation*.

15   Rabbi Menachem Mendel Schneerson, *Derech Mitzvosecha* (New York: Sichos in English, 2004), pp. 14-17.

The Right Words at the Right Times

Certain times of day are most appropriate for certain prayers.

In the Chabad *siddur*, the sentence "I hereby take upon myself the mitzvah of loving my fellow as myself," is recited every morning at the start of the daily prayers. It is followed by the verse (Numbers 24:5), "How goodly are your tents, O Jacob."

That verse was originally uttered by the evil prophet Bilaam, who intended to curse the Israelites as he had been hired to do by Balak, the Moabite king. Instead, Bilaam blessed them, at G-d's command. Our sages teach that the word "goodly" refers to the fact that the Israelites in the desert arranged their tents so that the entrances would not face each other and no one would be able to see into his neighbor's home. According to the Baal Shem Tov, this means that the Jews did not scrutinize their neighbors' faults.

These two statements are juxtaposed in the *siddur* to remind us that we can attain a true love of our fellow Jew by overlooking his flaws and focusing instead on fixing ourselves. When we elevate ourselves, we influence others to make positive changes of their own. If you happen to peek into someone else's "tent" and see a flaw, realize that this apparently negative character trait is actually a misdirection of the soul's great potential for holiness.

First, draw that flaw back to its source of holiness. Doing so will help you see the good within that person, even if it is buried deep.

Second, look into your own "tent" and examine your own faults.

The best time to take an accounting of your deeds and your progress is at night, before going to sleep. Ending your day without reviewing your personal account is like lying down in filthy clothes and wearing them again the next day. The "dirt" of your unrectified actions accumulates on your soul, layer upon layer, making it increasingly difficult to "get clean"—that is, to start the day with a refreshed spirit, renewed enthusiasm, and a positive outlook.

To understand yourself and the people around you properly, it is important to have an insight into human personality. This can be gained by knowledge of the four elements which determine our makeup.

Four Elements of Creation

According to Jewish philosophy,[16] G-d created the world using four elements: earth, fire, water, and air. The *Zohar* (*Vaera* 23b) explains that these elements are an expression of the four letters of G-d's holy name. From these four

16 Articulated by many different Sages and philosophers, particularly 15th century kabbalist Rabbi Chaim Vital. For further insight into the elements of personality, see my *Let's Go Camping* (New York: Writer's Press, 2007).

elements, G-d created every physical being. Obviously, as each person is different, in each person these elements are present in differing amounts. Identifying the predominant element in our personality can help us to understand and best utilize our essential strengths and weaknesses.

Each element must be balanced and used in the proper way in order to be beneficial. Please refer to my CD, "The Four Elements and You,"[17] for an in-depth discussion of each element as it relates to personality. *Tanya* (Chapter 1) explains the influence these elements have on our character traits.

Earth is low, heavy, and immobile; this element directs a person toward contemplation, considered analysis, stoicism, and introspection. It can also lead to laziness, sadness, and despair. The main weakness in Earth personalities is that they do not push themselves to accomplish or grow. The positive aspect of such a personality manifests in good judgment, loyalty, humility, cooperation, reliability, and trustworthiness.

Fire rises and flames consume. A Fire personality strives for the top. From their higher vantage point, Fire personalities can visualize a complex canvas and judge the possible outcomes of various paths. They are willing and able to take responsibility, to lead, and to achieve. The negative expressions of this personality type are the explosive character flaws of arrogance, anger, criticism and condescension toward others; the ability to take control

---

17   Available online from Kehot Publication Society.

can become an overwhelming desire for power. On the positive side, Fire can be used to warm one's heart and it can be channeled into serving G-d with a fiery passion; Fire personalities can reach great heights of prayer and learning and love of G-d.

Water has no innate boundaries; it must be contained by an external receptacle. A Water person "goes with the flow," spreading out wherever access leads. They are easygoing and loving, able to give of themselves and to help others grow. The negative manifestations of a Water personality may be instability, a lack of self-control, and a lack of judgment; following the path of least resistance often leads to a life of physical excess and addictions. Water-dominant people, never feeling they have enough, have a need to amass possessions. This desire can be channeled in a positive way towards the acquisition of more Torah and *mitzvos*.

Air is invisible, everywhere and anywhere, impossible to pin down. An Air person is a wonderful source of ideas and idealism, and yearns to follow the spiritual, transcendent path. Air-dominant people are not particularly concerned with physical realities or needs. Routine is uncomfortable to them. They may find it difficult to stick with a chosen path, and will flit from one position to another. An Air person is also very involved with the power of speech, whose source is air. They are able to speak well and convincingly, and can use words in holy ways to help others—e.g., as teachers, rabbis, therapists—but may abuse this ability by speaking aimlessly or harmfully.

Determining which trait defines you or your spouse will take time and careful analysis; it may not be obvious which trait predominates. In some people, two or more traits may be equally dominant. Knowing one's tendencies, though, makes it easier to deal with and direct them. Once you understand your character, you will be better able to refine it.

Rise Above the Waters

In addition to prayer (which, as noted earlier, primarily affects one's emotions), learning Torah and fulfilling its mitzvos are means by which to accomplish this refinement of character. They will affect the intellectual and physical aspects of one's character. The Lubavitcher Rebbe explains the Talmudic statement (*Kidushin* 30b) that G-d created the Torah as *tavlin* ("spices" or "antidote") to the *yetzer hara* to mean that "learning Torah is a spice to sweeten the *yetzer hara* into a *yetzer hatov*."[18]

In the Torah portion discussing the flood, Noach (Noah) is described (Genesis 6:9, 7:1) as "a righteous man in his generation." This phrase is explained to mean that if Noach had been born in a different generation, he would

18   Rabbi Israel Baal Shem Tov, *Tzava'at Harivash*, translated and annotated by J. Immanuel Schochet (New York: Kehot Publication Society, 1998), 138.

not have been considered, when he came into the world, to be a *tzaddik*. But he worked hard on himself, and Noach became a *tzaddik*. This teaches us that we too can work on ourselves to reach that higher level.

The *mayim rabim*, the "great waters" raging around the ark, can be seen as a metaphor for all the troubles and tribulations we experience in our lives that we sometimes feel are drowning us: the challenges of being married, the challenges of raising children, the challenges of taking care of ourselves.

The Hebrew word *teivah*, "ark," can also mean "word." Through the words of Torah and the words of *tefillah*, prayer, you can build an ark for yourself, a means of protection against all the raging waters, against all our emotional, intellectual and physical trials and tribulations.

And on this *teivah* you must have a window. A window that will allow the G-dly light to come streaming through, to banish the darkness in your heart—your negative energies, your anxiety, your depression—with Hashem's Torah and *mitzvos*.

Go to the Real You

In the following Torah portion, *Lech Lecha*, Avram (Abram) is asked (Genesis 12:1) to leave from not one but three places. Hashem tells him, "*lech lecha*, go to you." The word *lech*, "go," is almost the same as *lecha*, "to you." Why is it written as an apparent repetition, instead of, for example, *lech leatzmecha*, "go to yourself"? Avram is told to leave his country, his birthplace, and the house of his father, to set out for an unknown destination and leave these familiar places behind, perhaps forever. In doing so, Avram will fulfill his potential and become Avraham (Abraham) the Patriarch.

What is the distinction between homeland, birthplace, and family home? Why did Avraham have to abandon these three specific things? There are three particulars that even modern psychology says can induce a person into giving up.[19]

The first is *artzecha*, "your land." Land in Hebrew is *eretz*, which comes from the two-letter rootword *ratz*, to run. Running indicates a will to go somewhere. If this will is not applied properly, if it is not directed towards a spiritual goal, it deteriorates into a desire for escapism and a development of dysfunctional coping mechanisms that distract you from reaching your true potential.

The second is *moladitcha*, "your birthplace." This represents a person's genetic predisposition, the particular temperament with which you were born.

The third one is *bais avicha*, "your father's house"—the environment in which you were raised. You may feel that your childhood was lacking in the nurturing necessary for you to become a loving person, and consequently you do not have the emotional resources to be a successful spouse and parent. But this is not true. As Avram is shown, it is possible

19   Rabbi Sholom Dov Ber Schneerson, *Kuntres Ha'avoda: Love Like Fire and Water*, ed. Rabbi Dovid Sterne (New York: Moznaim Press, 2011).

to leave the past behind; to detach yourself from the way in which you were raised and go to the real you, the you that is loving and patient and kind and possessed of spiritual energy.

Thus, to achieve real growth, one may have to overcome childhood environment, genetic predisposition, and/or ingrained habits. But take heart from the Torah to believe that even if you were not born or raised as a *tzaddik*, or you habitually do not behave like one, you do possess the innate ability to raise yourself to a higher spiritual level.

G-dly Imagination

There are many words in the Hebrew language for "man," but in *Chassidic* terminology, *adam* refers to the highest level that a human can achieve. An *adam* possesses the *koach hadimyon*, the faculty of imagination and intellectual expansion. A person who can expand his mind has a greater ability to be *medameh*, "similar to" Hashem. G-d gave us this faculty of imagination to be used to draw ourselves close to Him.

This faculty needs to be developed—or in most cases, rectified—with concerted effort. An unrectified imagination "inevitably leads one toward apathy, lethargy, or despair. The untamed imagination is therefore the psychological base of one's evil inclination, the ultimate goal of which is to lead man into the abyss of depression and apathy."[20]

Direct Your Imagination— Or It Will Direct You

If we do not tap into this true source of goodness, then the *yetzer hara* uses it against us to make associations between things that are not based on reality. Thoughts such as "I can't cope with my spouse anymore!" or "I deserve better!" creep into one's mind. When a person's imagination runs wild it causes havoc, mental confusion, and distortion of reality, because "based on faulty structures woven by the imagination, the mind will proceed to draw spurious inferences (an extreme example being the psychosis of paranoia)."[21]

Conversely, when we direct our imagination in a holy endeavor, such as when we meditate in our prayers on G-dliness or when we learn Torah, we rectify the wild imagination within us. The *Frierdiker* Rebbe recounts in his memoirs[22] that his father, the Rebbe Rashab, frequently tested him with intellectual games to develop his

---

20   Ginsburgh, page 49.

21   Ibid, p. 59.

22   Rabbi Yosef Yitzchak Schneersohn, *Likkutei Dibburim*, translated by Uri Kaploun (New York: Kehot Publication Society, 1987).

imagination, saying that the young boy would need it in his service to Hashem.

Self-Control Is Our Goal

G-d has placed us here on earth to strengthen the inclination of our Divine souls to do good, and resist the efforts of our *yetzer hara* to ensnare us into succumbing to our animalistic drives. Simply put, our job is to gain self-control.

One day as I was out walking, I noticed a blind person accompanied by a guide dog. It occurred to me that if a seeing-eye dog can be trained to overcome its instincts in order to guide a blind person, surely human beings can train themselves to overcome harmful instincts and habits. Not only do we have greater mental capacity than an animal, but G-d has provided us with many resources to help us in this endeavor of self-improvement: a superior intellect, a G-dly soul, and the Torah as a manual to guide us.

With these tools, we can work from the outside in and from the inside out, to change the way we behave and the way we think.

Exercises and Meditations

Evaluate the expectations you have for yourself. Consider your responsibilities and your available time. Are your expectations realistic? If not, adjust them to your reality. If necessary, decrease your demands on yourself and place limits on the demands made on you by others.

Accept upon yourself only goals that can actually be accomplished without overwhelming you. If you feel torn between wanting to spend every second of the day with your children and trying to find time to pray, be creative and find ways to fit both into your schedule. For example, when my children were infants, if I didn't wake up early enough to pray on my own, I would pray with them or I would wait until they napped and finish my prayers at that time.

Once you have set some goals for yourself, note your progress regularly. Remember that progress may be slow, but every step counts. Visualize a baby taking its first steps. See yourself smiling at the baby's wobbling efforts. See yourself applauding the baby. Notice that the baby seems very satisfied with its progress, and may even applaud its own efforts. It is not discouraged by frequent falls. Visualize yourself making progress in baby steps. Smile at yourself, as you would smile at a baby. Applaud yourself—mentally or actually, with some small reward—for your efforts. Be patient with yourself. Do not be discouraged if you falter.

Visualize yourself during *tefillah* as a car at a gas station, filling up on all three intellectual powers. There is no limit to how much you can take, or to how much Hashem can expand your intelligence and your mindfulness.

Devote some time to determining your predominant characteristic. Be aware that many people have two or even all four elements dominant. Realize that one trait may be easier to rectify than another, which may require many years of personal work. Set up a plan to utilize your strengths in your areas of challenge. (This will be discussed further in the next chapter.)

Ask yourself, "What element in myself and what element in my spouse makes us susceptible to certain negative traits?" Imagine different ways in which you could help strengthen yourself and your spouse to overcome those traits.

When the demands upon you seem overwhelming, visualize yourself in an ark, rising safely above the raging waters.

Three exercises can help achieve further expansion of the mind: 1) *Hitbodedut*, solitude: training yourself to be alone with Hashem. 2) *Iyun* (or *hitbonenut*): contemplation, taking the time to thoroughly investigate and understand what you are learning, through focused review. 3) *Hitakvut*, deliberation: focusing your attention on the subject matter to the exclusion of everything else.

The morning is the best time of day to perform any meditative exercise, but maximum concentration at any time will be beneficial. Merely mouthing the words of *tefillah* or the *Tanya* of the day will not suffice. Reading the words out loud will increase your concentration. Try to think of the meaning of the words as you say them.

For at least five minutes a day, read aloud a portion of the daily prayers or a chapter of Psalms in a language you understand, as though you are speaking to Hashem. Then use your own words to tell Hashem about an issue with which you are struggling. Consider the issue from different angles. Focus only on one issue at a time.

Points for Practical Reflection

- The goal of a married couple is to regain that level of unity they had in heaven.

- When we strive to achieve that unity, G-d helps us also achieve the personal transformation to which we aspire.

- Improving our character will improve our relationships.

- It is possible to change our instincts and patterns.

- A bamboo plant takes years to grow roots, but the plant flourishes to great heights in weeks.

- Be patient with yourself and those you love.

- We may turn to G-d for all our needs, material and spiritual.

- We may have absolute faith that with G-d's help we will achieve our goal.

- Focused prayer expands our mind and refines our emotions.

- Four different elements, in infinite combination, form the basis of our personality.

- Determining the dominant element in our personality helps us to know our strengths and weaknesses.

- Learning Torah helps us rise above the turmoil in our lives.

- Increased *bitachon* makes it easier for you to be patient with yourself and others.

3

—

Introspection And Restraint

It is common for us to note the flaws of others. Sometimes we ignore them, sometimes we address them directly, sometimes we approach the topic with caution and tact. Each reaction may be appropriate at some specific time, but the last is usually the wisest course.

Once upon a time, a competition was held for the best portrait of the king. Unfortunately, the king was ugly: short and hunchbacked, with bulging eyes, a clubfoot, and a blemish on his cheek.

The first contestant, who hoped to flatter the king, depicted him as tall and handsome. The king exclaimed, "Are you mocking me?" and he banished the hapless subject.

The next contestant, who prided himself on his honesty, painted the king exactly as he appeared. The king exclaimed, "You have insulted me!" and this unfortunate artist was also banished.

The third contestant portrayed the king realistically, but in such a way that no one could detect any deformities. He painted the king seated on his horse, leaning over with a rifle in his hand, as if at a hunt. Because he was bent over, one could not see that he had a hunchback. Because he was squinting at his target, one could not see that his eyes bulged. And since the portrait displayed only one side of the king, one could not see his clubfoot or the blemish on his face.

Beauty is indeed in the eyes of the beholder. We have the ability to perceive any person and any situation in a positive way, if we choose to do so.

Negative Is Potentially Positive

Similarly, you can train yourself to perceive your own and your spouse's attributes realistically, yet positively. Both husband and wife should strive to accept the other's imperfections. The first step toward achieving this goal is to maintain a high level of self-awareness.

You can more readily discern the potential good in yourself and your spouse, when you realize that every negative attribute is simply an unrectified positive attribute. After determining your dominant personality trait, as discussed in the preceding chapter, utilize it for good. For example, as mentioned, a person who has a fiery temperament can channel that fire toward a passion for *davening*, a passion for learning, a passion for helping people, for loving his fellow Jews and loving Hashem. A person whose earthy temperament inclines her toward depression can channel her introspection to a thorough investigation of a difficult decision.

Once you have overcome a negative trait, you will be able to attain a loftier spiritual height than someone who was never tried with that negative attribute in the first place. As we are taught (*Berachos* 34b), "In the place where penitents stand, even the wholly righteous cannot stand."

Not OK Is Also OK

Even as you wonder, "When will my spouse start to improve?" he or she may be thinking the same thing about you. You might both wait endlessly for the other person to make the first move—and you may find yourself still waiting fifty years later, G-d forbid.

It is imperative to realize that no person is always 100% OK—and that is OK. Only angels are perfect. Although we may sometimes violate our own standards of how a person should behave, we must still accept and love ourselves. Our setbacks do not define who we are. Growth is a life-long process; human beings are not created at the level of an angel.

G-d sees each individual as a sublimely beautiful soul. You may not feel that way about yourself. Your conduct may more often than not fall far short of His standards. But despite your failings, G-d focuses on the beauty of your holy soul and loves you unconditionally. Just as a parent loves his child even when the child misbehaves, so too G-d loves you and always seeks to be close to you. It is up to us to follow G-d's lead, and see beyond a person's present shortcomings to the beauty of their inner soul.

Accept Your Partner's Faults

To a woman who had complained about her husband's faults, the Lubavitcher Rebbe wrote:

...Until after the arrival of Moshiach, there is no person without a fault. Hence, just as one person has a fault, it is certain that so, too, the other has a fault. And just as one does not want to uncover and highlight one's [own] fault, one should also not highlight and magnify another's fault. This is how things should be between Jews in general; how much more

so when the person under discussion is your husband and the father of your child.

My aim here is not to rebuke, but to make you aware that your situation is not as harsh as you perceive it to be, nor is it exceptional, as you imagine it to be. Each of you should overlook things, preferring to find ways of establishing domestic harmony. And once domestic harmony reigns, this is the vessel into which G-d pours blessing, and success, and good health, and livelihood, and blissful contentment ... [from] one's children....

Perhaps you are guilty of the same offense toward your spouse that you feel your spouse is perpetrating against you.

Honest self-analysis will enable you to take note when you have fallen short and resolve to take the necessary steps to correct yourself.

The Pot Calling the Kettle Black

The Talmud teaches (*Bava Basra* 60b) that the repetition in the verse (Leviticus 19:17) "Rebuke, you shall rebuke" indicates that one ought to correct one's own faults before correcting those faults in someone else. When you notice any deficiency in your spouse, remind yourself that a negative quality one sees in another may be a reflection of something in oneself that requires rectification.

The previous Rebbe writes[23]:

23   *Likkutei Dibburim*, vol. 5, page 82.

The first step in the direction of serving G-d must be the fulfillment of the verse, "And you shall eradicate the evil from your midst." ... The trouble is that there is a prevalent fault: people are often very fond of themselves. A person in this situation does not find faults within himself. Even if he does somehow sense that not everything is exactly as it ought to be, he has a ready battery of extenuating explanations. Indeed, he may even come to regard himself as a man of stature.

How, then, can one know if he has any evil within himself? The answer is in the verse, "Your evil will chastise you": a man is oppressed by the evil within himself. It can happen that when one notes something evil in another, not only does he not give him the benefit of the doubt, but he finds himself perturbed by what he perceives as severe guilt. He may even speak about this publicly. (In truth, of course, one's fellow should be rebuked lovingly and privately.) Indeed, from his words one may observe that he in fact is pained by what he perceives. In truth, however, what is really bothering him is the evil within himself.

Instead of focusing on each other's faults, a couple should try to perceive and draw out the good in each other.

They should emulate Rabbi Levi Yitzchok of Berdichev, who was "legendary for petitioning G-d for mercy whenever the Jewish people were in danger. Time and again he would advocate on behalf of his fellow Jews and remind G-d of their many merits that made them worthy of salvation. Even when it was apparent to all that a Jew had sinned, Rabbi Levi Yitzchok always managed to find a defense for the sinner, pointing out the person's good qualities and good intentions.... Rabbi Levi Yitzchok had risen to the level where he truly perceived the good within every Jew."[24]

Make Peace with Imperfection

Keep in mind that beyond all the pragmatic benefits of improved relationships, *shalom bayis* is a *mitzvah* for the purpose of perfecting the soul. The reason that the Jewish people gave the *korbon shlamim* (peace offering) soon after *matan Torah* (receiving the Torah) was because they had reached a spiritual state of elevation. G-d was symbolically preparing His people in the desert for their future involvement in a more mundane life. In this way they would become accustomed to sacrifice perfectionism and learn to be at peace with the process of attaining completion.

Shalom is, essentially, making peace with our own and others' inadequacies.

Look in Your Own Pocket First

It is necessary to recognize and attempt to rectify your own inadequacies before working on someone else's. As we mentioned in the previous chapter, look in your own tent first—or in your own pockets, as in the following story,

24 Ibid.

47

told often by Reb Mendel Futerfas, famed *chasid* of the Lubavitcher Rebbe:

> *I had been imprisoned in a Soviet labor camp for teaching Torah. In the barracks, the hardened criminals regularly played cards, although the possession of such an amenity was strictly forbidden. On occasion, a guard would drop by in an effort to confiscate the deck of cards, but incredibly he was never able to find it.*
>
> *One day, I asked one of the card players how they always managed to hide the deck. The inmate responded: "We are experienced thieves and we have quick hands. When a guard comes in, we slip the cards into his pocket. That is the one place he would never think of looking. And when he leaves, we slip the cards out again."*

Just as the guard never thought to look inside his own pockets, we tend not to search our own "pockets" of imperfection but instead look into the "pockets" of those around us. Were we to look in our own pockets, at our own flaws, we would realize that change is not easy. And once we accepted that, we would be more patient with others and less eager to criticize them.

Speak Softly

When you do offer criticism, it must be without anger. King Solomon teaches (Proverbs 15:1) that "A gentle answer turns away wrath, but a harsh word stirs up anger." If you speak in anger, generally you will be answered with anger. To succeed in your mission to help your spouse and increase the peace in your home, you need to speak calmly and kindly. As the Zohar states (*Tikkunim* 69:2), "One who carefully guards himself against giving in to anger and avoids any arguments, merits that his home is compared to the Holy Temple."

The Lubavitcher Rebbe addresses this point by using the story of the staff of Aharon (Aaron), told in Exodus (7:9-13): When Moshe (Moses) and Aharon appeared before Pharaoh, Aharon threw down his staff and it turned into a snake. Pharaoh's magicians did the same with their own staffs. Then Aharon's staff swallowed up all the other staffs. Our sages explicate (*Shabbos* 97a) that Aharon's staff didn't swallow the other staffs when it was in the form of a snake but, even more wondrously, when it was in its natural shape as an inanimate rod.

The Lubavitcher Rebbe teaches[25]:

Generally, one should draw another Jew closer to Judaism only by showing him love and care. Sometimes, however, it appears necessary to speak with him more strongly, for his own sake, i.e., to "swallow" him up. At that point one should remember:

a) That "swallowing" is done with the staff of Aharon, who was renowned for his love for the Jewish people. Therefore, even in a moment of rebuke, a person must be extremely careful

25 Miller, Exodus 2:42.

not to involve any personal anger. Rather, the "swallowing" should be purely for the benefit of the recipient.

b) The swallowing should not be done while the staff is a snake, i.e. not through venomous anger, but with the solid resolve ("staff") of a responsible educator.

In his commentary on the ethical essay of the Ramban (Rabbi Moshe ben Nachman, Nachmanides) to his son, *A Letter for the Ages*, Rabbi Avraham Chaim Feuer expresses it well[26]: "Gentle words have more force than crescendos of indignation."

Kindness of Control

Controlling our anger is beneficial on every plane. Not only does it ensure that our human relationships in this world will improve, but it guarantees a closer relationship to G-d, as the Talmud states more than once: "The entire world exists only in the merit of the person who restrains his words at the time of a quarrel" (*Chullin* 89a), and "Three people are especially beloved by G-d: One who does not lose control of his temper, one who does not become drunk, and one who does not demand his full rights" (*Pesachim* 113a).

---

26 Rabbi Avrohom Chaim Feuer, *Iggeres HaRamban: Letter for the Ages* (New York: ArtScroll, 1989) p. 27. The Ramban (1194-1270) was a leading Spanish Talmudist, philosopher, kabbalist, biblical commentator, physician, and communal leader.

This is the true test. Those who are capable of controlling their emotions, those who can be tempted and yet restrain themselves, are strong like the sun. Those who do not answer back, who are internally quiet in the midst of turmoil, will merit to reach a very high level of piety and humility and closeness to Hashem.

And they will reap additional reward for their restraint. Their act of "removing" their emotions will be mirrored in the future by G-d, when He will remove the shields that are hiding Him from our world. When He reveals Himself to the world, those who controlled themselves will experience a greater degree of revelation.

Swallow Your Words

While the surest path to *shalom bayis* is kindness, the second most important characteristic needed to achieve peace in the home—indeed, to benefit any personal relationship—is to become proficient in the art of silence.

Reishis Chochmah[27] advises silence as an antidote to anger.[28] The Rebbe's advice to "swallow" the person whom we wish to rebuke can also relate to ourselves: we need to learn to swallow our words before they cause damage.

---

27 A classic ethical work compiled in 1575 by Eliyahu de Vidas, a disciple of the sixteenth century kabbalist, Rabbi Moshe Cordovero.

28 Rabbi Shalom Dov Ber Schneersohn, *Yom Tov Shel Rosh Hashanah 5659, a Chassidic Discourse,* translated and annotated by Rabbi Yosef B. Marcus and Rabbi Moshe Miller (New York: Kehot Publication Society, 2000) p. 33.

There are times when you may feel that you just cannot be kind to your spouse. Well, if you can't be kind, be quiet!

It has often been pointed out that the letters of the word "listen" can be rearranged to spell "silent" —a reminder that in order to do the first, one has to be the second. How often have you responded angrily or impetuously, and then wished you could snatch your words back out of the air? How often have you had to apologize, when it would have been so much easier had you just kept quiet? From the other perspective, how often have you bitten your lip instead of replying, and then realized that not answering saved you from a terrible scene? How often has your spouse said to you, sincerely, "Thanks for listening"?

If the former happens much more frequently than the latter, it will be very helpful for you to learn to master the art of silence.

The Power of Speech

Hashem created people as *medabrim*, speakers. Why would He choose to focus on that characteristic rather than on any another prominent human trait—for example, why not focus on our intellect and instead call us *sichli*, intellectuals? (This may explain why we often speak before we think.)

The Lubavitcher Rebbe explained[29] that speech differs from thought in one dramatic way: words travel from the personal, internal domain of the speaker into the external, public world outside of the speaker. A person's thoughts exist only within his or her own mind, until they are translated into verbal communication and attain a separate existence.

Speech is extremely powerful. Humans, unlike the rest of creation, are endowed with the ability to build goodness and kindness in the world through our words. We can speak words of love, of kindness, of friendship, of comfort, of joy.[30] Many forms of speech are considered holy: prayer, Torah reading and learning, blessings, words of consolation.

Silence is Kindness

Yet silence is healthy for us spiritually and physically. Our Sages said (Ethics of the Fathers 1:17), "Shimon [ben Gamliel] said, 'All my days I have been raised among the sages and I have found nothing better for the body than silence; ... he who is profuse of words causes sin.'"

We have an unlimited amount of breath to use to say good things. We are, however, limited regarding speaking

29   *Likkutei Sichos*, vol. 4 *Avos* ch. 1; from an address on *Shabbos Parshas Acharei Mos*, 24 Nissan, 5719 (May 2, 1959).

30   Rebbetzin Holly Pavlov, *Mirrors of Our Lives: Reflections of Women in Tanach* (Jerusalem: Targum Press, 2000) p. 77 (see pp. 62-78 in that book for an in-depth treatment of this topic).

vanities or worse. The Talmud (*Megillah* 18a) states that "Speech is worth one coin, but silence is worth two." Our words should be even more precious to us than our coins, and we must be even more careful in how we use them.

There are numerous indicators in Tanach and Talmud linking silence to peace. *Tanya*[31] states that Gd created the world with speech; when He stopped speaking, our peaceful *Shabbos* came into existence. The Talmud (*Shabbos* 116a), discussing the situation of a woman accused of immoral behavior, who is prohibited to her husband until her innocence is proven,[32] says that "G-d says: 'Let My Name, written in sanctity, be blotted out to make peace between a man and his wife!'"

We can follow Hashem's lead; we can keep silent to create a peaceful home. If Hashem can erase His name for *shalom bayis,* can't we take the extra precaution and stop speaking for a moment?

Silence is Strength

The Gemara (*Chullin* 89a) recommends that we pursue silence throughout our life: "What is man's task in the

31 *Kuntres Acharon,* p. 400.

32 During the time of the Beis HaMikdash, a married woman suspected of infidelity (a *Sotah*) would be asked to drink water in which a portion of the Torah containing several mentions of G-d's name had been soaked, erasing the words. If the water had no adverse effect on her, she was considered innocent and her marriage was still valid.

world? To make himself silent." In order to do so, we should act as if we are deaf. The goal is to control our reaction to certain statements, to behave as if we had not even heard them.

When Aharon the High Priest heard of the death of his sons Nadav and Avihu—killed by the fire of G-d's breath for doing holy work improperly—he kept silent. For this he was highly praised.

Often our weakest point is reached through speech: when certain people say certain things to us, we are strongly tempted to defend ourselves by retorting in a similar—or usually worse—manner. Our ego is activated and it becomes difficult to control our tongues.

It is difficult for others to judge our silence. Even if they are deeply involved with our situation, no one can know for sure what we choose not to say. But we know, and we know the effort it took to stay silent. And Hashem knows, too.

One woman recorded in a journal her every instance of verbal self-restraint, because she believed that every time she resisted the temptation to answer defensively or hurtfully, she increased goodness in the world. In her will, she stated that she wanted the journal to be buried with her.

It is not, however, necessary nor healthy to keep quiet if you will then stew resentfully in your silence. Casting yourself in the role of a silent martyr will not help your relationship. If there is an issue you wish to address or some statement you wish to make, you should express yourself—in the right way and at the right time, calmly, and not in the heat of the moment.

One way to remind ourselves of this is during our prayers, when we recite the *Amidah* (*Shemone Esray*, Silent Meditation), at the end. (Please see the exercises following this and later chapters for practical guidance on this point.)

Silent Connection

We often use words to build a barrier around us. Although "the silent treatment"—which I never recommend—is often used as payback to express our negative feelings toward others, silence can be used in positive ways.

Silence can create an entryway through that barrier of words. Through that entryway, we allow G-d and love to enter our hearts. When we pause and choose to listen rather than to speak, with a humble demeanor and compassion in our eyes and body language, we show that we care what our partner has to say. As the Rebbe pointed out[33], "Many are the sayings of our Sages, including also our Rebbes of saintly memory, which urge husband and wife always to discuss matters of mutual concern, and to give patient attention to the opinion of the other...."

---

33 *Letters from the Rebbe*, p. 192.

The verse in Psalms (50:8) says, "Indeed, in silence speak righteousness; judge uprightly the sons of men." How can one speak in silence? By thinking first and considering the significance of the words we are bringing into the world. As Rebbetzin Holly Pavlov writes, "The silence of righteousness is not empty; it creates a space for G-d. ...All of the speech that is important in this world should be defined by the silent thought process that goes into the speech. Speech should be defined ... by aligning our speech with G-d's will."[34]

The story of Eliyahu (Elijah) the prophet and his encounter with the Holy Presence (I Kings 19:9-12) is well-known. Eliyahu fled to Mount Sinai when he felt that his efforts to bring the Jewish people back to G-d were failing. There, G-d spoke to him and told him to stand before Him on the mountain. As Eliyahu stands exposed on the mountaintop, a mighty wind passes by, followed by a violent earthquake and then a blazing fire. But "G-d was not in the wind," nor in the earthquake, nor in the fire. Finally, after all the bombastic events, came "a still, small voice."

And in that still small voice was G-d's presence.

The story seems to come to teach us that had Eliyahu spoken more quietly, the people would have listened. When we are silent, we can hear that voice of G-d. When we choose to speak less, we can be heard more. One who has mastered the art of silence will know when to speak and when to keep quiet.

34 Pavlov, p. 74.

Exercises and Meditations

Recognize the positive in yourself: Write down three positive qualities you have. Recall the positive effect utilizing those qualities has on those around you. Then write down three positive qualities you wish you had. Visualize yourself possessing those qualities. Visualize yourself acting in a manner consistent with those positive traits. Visualize the positive effect mastering those qualities can have on your life.

Now consider that your spouse possesses positive qualities that complement your own. Acknowledge the positive qualities your spouse possesses, and the beneficial effects that accompany them. Write them down. Then write down three positive qualities you wish your spouse possessed. Visualize him or her mastering those qualities and acting in a manner consistent with those positive traits. Visualize the positive effect that could have on your life together.

Strive to accept imperfections in yourself and your spouse. Identify a negative character trait that you possess and one that your spouse possesses. Envision yourself applying this trait in a positive way. Map out the steps you think would be necessary for you to make that happen.

Increase your awareness of how your speech might be contributing to tension in your marital relationship. Ask yourself questions such as, "Did I speak in a refined manner today? Did I get anxious when my spouse seemed angry or critical with me? Was I spiteful? Did I sound condescending?"

Note the instances in which you restrained yourself from an angry, impulsive, or critical comment. Note the positive effects this restraint engendered—even if they seem minimal. You may want to keep a written record of these instances.

Points For Practical Reflection

- Often the fault you find in others, is your own.

- Recognizing and trying to correct your own character flaws increases your patience for others and their flaws.

- Be honest but compassionate when you examine your faults.

- If you can love yourself despite your imperfections, you can love your spouse despite his or her imperfections.

- Your efforts at self-improvement will influence your spouse to make positive changes as well.

- Negative character traits can be seen as indications of one's high-level soul and the potential spiritual heights one can attain.

- Accepting criticism calmly and thoughtfully reduces the likelihood of being criticized in the future.

- Silence is sometimes the best response.

4

Working From the Outside In—Doing Kindness

When a couple comes to me for marriage counseling, I tell them the Alter Rebbe's teaching[35] that one should train oneself to act in a positive manner even if one doesn't feel like doing so. In this way, a person attains a new pattern of behavior that becomes second nature. According to the Alter Rebbe, this is not a transformation, but a return to one's true self.

As I was riding in a taxi to Manhattan once to give a *shiur*, reviewing my notes, I was shaken out of my quiet mood when the driver slammed on the brakes. My head

35 *Tanya* Chapt. 14 (end)

snapped up and I found myself staring at a billboard emblazoned with the phrase, "*I am because I do.*" My first thought was, "That is so *Chassidish.*" Analyzing it a bit more, I realized that the message is true, but only partially. *I am* also because I *don't* do. For instance, when I refrain from speaking harmful words, *I am* as much the real me as when *I am* saying positive things. In reality, "I am because I do speak, and I am because I don't speak."

Stop Thinking and Act

The Lubavitcher Rebbe was once consulted by a female university student who had some obnoxious habits that prevented her from getting along with others. She had undergone psychotherapy for several years, but this did not solve her problems. She presented the Rebbe with eight pages of self-analysis, but he set it aside and gave her a simple piece of advice: "When you return to school, in the dining room make it a habit to become aware of what other people need and bring them those items."

In other words, even if she was not intrinsically nice, she should act nice. To that end, she should stop analyzing herself and instead accustom herself to think, speak, and behave considerately.

Acting Leads to Being

There is a well-known rabbinic phrase (cf. *Yoma* 72b), "The inner (soul) follows the outer (behavior)." A common adaptation of this is "Fake it till you make it." The way you act becomes the way you are. If you wish to change, you need to pattern a behavior until it becomes internalized.

The Ramban writes in his famous letter of ethical instruction to his son, "Accustom yourself to speak gently to all people at all times."[36] The phrase "accustom yourself" tells us that this behavior can be achieved with thought and time. Rabbi Feuer advises: "Be prepared. Don't let unnerving situations catch you by surprise. Before crisis hits, prepare in your mind how you would like to react to trying situations, and resolve to make every effort not to surrender to panic or rage."

It is inevitable that at times, you will deal with people and events that could cause you stress or pain. Many of our responses to stressful situations are habitual. It is important that you recognize and then change these responses. You need to work on training yourself to react in a calm way to difficult situations and difficult people, rather than reacting thoughtlessly out of habit, with impatience or anger.

36 Feuer, p. 27.

Practice, Practice, Practice

The concept of retraining mental habits is touched upon in Jewish law with reference to changing one of the blessings in the *Amidah*, the central prayer, at springtime. At that period, the phrase *mashiv haruach umorid hageshem* ("He causes the wind to blow and brings down the rain") is replaced with *morid hatal* ("He brings down the dew"). We are told that the average person requires a full month, i.e. ninety verbal repetitions of the new formulation, to fully adjust to the change.[37]

Let me share something that happened in my own life that illustrates how challenging it can be to act consciously when we are used to engaging in routine activities.

It was Elul, the month before the High Holidays, and many guests were staying in our home. It is quite common in Crown Heights for guests to stay from the beginning of Elul until the end of Succos—nearly two months. They come to prepare themselves spiritually for the High Holidays and celebrate Rosh Hashanah, Yom Kippur, Succos, Shemini Atzeres, and Simchas Torah in the heart of the Chabad community.

Our guests were staying in the room in which I kept posted the phone numbers of the stores and services I regularly use. Whenever I needed a telephone number, I would have to go into that room. Of course I knocked first,

---

37 *Hilchos Yom Tov* and *Hilchos Tefilah*, of the Alter Rebbe's *Shulchan Aruch*, 114:10.

but almost invariably, I disturbed my guests' sleep, for which I felt quite guilty.

After a week of this, it suddenly dawned on me to just remove the list from the guest room and tape it up in my kitchen. (Perhaps it took so long to figure this out just to drive home this lesson about habituation.)

But guess what? Even after moving the list, whenever I needed a number, I would *still* automatically go to the guests' room, knock, and peek inside. Except now I would wonder where the list had gone. It took another day or so until I remembered—as I stood at the door of that room, about to knock—where it was now. From then on, I began going automatically to the new spot.

This was a powerful lesson that acquiring a new routine requires repeated practice over a period of time to reprogram one's automatic response.

Smile on the Outside to Smile on the Inside

Rabbi Nachum Partzovitz (1923-1986), former head of Mir Yeshiva, was famous for greeting everyone with extraordinary friendliness, despite years of intense physical suffering. Once he was asked how he managed to smile despite his disabling pain. He replied by quoting Rav Yechiel Mordechai Gordon (1887 -1929), Rosh Yeshiva of Lomza,

Poland, who said that a person's face is public property. Just as Jewish law prohibits a person from leaving a hole in a public thoroughfare since it may endanger passersby, a person should never have an expression on his face that is likely to cause others discomfort.

I once read a story about a famous rabbi that emphasized this message[38]:

The rabbi was riding in an elevator in a small office building. As the door opened and another man entered, the rabbi remembered something that he had forgotten to do and in consequence he frowned. He soon left the elevator and the building, and got into the car that was waiting to take him to the airport. After riding just a few blocks—even though he was running late—the rabbi asked the driver to return to the building they had just left. The rabbi re-entered the building and searched room by room until he found the man he had seen briefly in the elevator. The rabbi took this man's hand and profusely apologized for having frowned. The man was visibly relieved and confided that he had indeed assumed that he had somehow offended the rabbi. The rabbi had realized correctly that the man had thought the frown was directed at him.

You are capable of internalizing the awareness that your face is "public property" so that you will develop the habit of presenting a pleasant face to the world. As you do so, you may find that your emotions are changing along with your

---

38   A similar story is told about Rabbi Moshe Feinstein in the book, *Reb Moshe: The Life and Ideals of HaGaon Rabbi Moshe Feinstein*, Rabbi Shimon Finkelman (New York: Mesorah Publications Ltd., 1986), p. 191-192.

demeanor. A pleasant expression can lead to a more pleasant disposition.

Focusing on a pleasant memory or kind action that was done to you will make it easier to maintain a smiling countenance. As you accustom yourself to smiling, it will become your natural habit. The smile on the outside will spread to a smile on the inside.

Kindness to Your Spouse Is Kindness to Yourself

The *Zohar* teaches that a soul may spend hundreds of years in the heavenly sphere awaiting the opportunity to descend to earth to perform one single mitzvah. The performance of mitzvos has a beneficial effect on both our spiritual and physical selves. As a Divinely created human being, you have an innate desire for spiritual harmony, and so doing good makes you feel good.

When you perform a *mitzvah*, you beautify and elevate your soul and improve your spiritual and physical well-being. This is true of any thoughtful act, even something as simple as greeting someone with a smile or saying a few warm words. Thus, any act of kindness you perform, even to someone who does not seem to deserve it—which at the moment may include your spouse—is an opportunity for you to refine yourself.

Rabbi Yossi Jacobson[39] tells a true story on this theme concerning a Holocaust survivor who currently lives in Crown Heights:

During World War II, when European Jews were rounded up by the Nazis and shipped by cattle car to concentration camps for extermination, this man was placed on such a train in the dead of winter. He was surrounded by emaciated Jews, freezing in the brutal cold. An elderly man next to him grabbed his arm and begged him to provide him with some warmth. The younger man began to rub the old man's frail body gently with his own cold hands. After a while, the muscles in his hands began to cramp and grew painful, and he wanted to stop rubbing, but every time he did so, the elderly man begged him to continue.

This went on throughout the night. At daybreak, the young man was astonished to discover that everyone in the cattle car had died of exposure except for the elderly man and himself. In the course of warming the old man's body, he had also warmed himself.

We learn from these stories that even when we think that we do not have the strength to help ourselves, we have enough strength for both ourselves and for others. It is precisely by helping someone else that we help ourselves. As recent studies have shown, cultivating a giving spirit contributes to one's health and longevity.[40]

---

39 Renowned lecturer and writer; transcriber of the Rebbe's sichos on his CD, "My Captain."

40 See *Likkutei Sichos* vol. 36 pg. 4ff.

Although you may at present find it challenging to bestow kindness on your spouse, do so anyway, for that will have a positive effect not only on him or her but on you as well. Ultimately, when you treat your spouse graciously and kindly, you draw the *Shechinah*, G-d's Presence, into yourself and gain its benefits.

Kindness Leads to Peace

In his book *Kindness*, Rabbi Zelig Pliskin maintains that "you are independent of how anyone else treats you. You are totally dependent on how you treat others."[41] Even if people do not treat you the way you wish to be treated, you can remain a positive person. You are free to shower others with kindness no matter how they treat you.

Acts of kindness generate positive energy. With your every act of kindness, you increase the peace in your home, and that leads to unlimited blessings. Our Sages teach (*Uktzin* 3:12) that "the Holy One, blessed be He, found no vessel that could contain blessing for Israel other than peace. As the verse states, 'G-d will give strength to His people; G-d will bless His people with peace' [Psalms 29:11]." Consequently, a husband and wife who create peace between themselves have each elevated their *neshamah* into a vessel worthy of receiving G-d's blessing.

---

41 Rabbi Zelig Pliskin, *Kindness: Changing People's Lives for the Better* (New York: Mesorah Publications Ltd, 2000), p. 130.

Unconditional Kindness

When I advise women to treat their husbands with unconditional kindness, some of them respond, "What! Treat my husband like he is a king? That would be letting him get away with murder! I am not such a *tzaddeikes* that I can overlook my husband's outrageous behavior and act nicely to him when he has been so mean to me."

Similarly, when I tell men to show unconditional kindness toward their wives, some of them complain, "You expect me to treat her like a princess when she treats me with such contempt?! Why, she even insults me in front of our children."

Nonetheless, continually finding fault with your spouse is likely to discourage him or her from trying to improve. Similarly, denigrating yourself for every misstep may lead you to give up on self-improvement. Being loving to your spouse—even if you have to force yourself to do so—likely will motivate him or her to continue to gain your approval by acting more considerately to you. And as that happens, you yourself are likely to feel more loving and act more kindly.

Critical Kindness

When you are the recipient of criticism, your immediate impulse may be to react defensively. But before you do so, first consider whether the criticism contains any truth. Second, recognize that your spouse probably made that observation because he or she wants you to be the best you can be. And third, even if your spouse's criticism reflects his or her feelings of insecurity rather than a desire to be constructive, and that criticism may provide your spouse with a perverse pleasure, be aware that when you respond calmly, thoughtfully, and pleasantly, you defuse the potentially hurtful situation before it brings you both down.

Your calm response will likely reduce the frequency of such criticism and, in addition, improve the emotional climate so that when your spouse offers criticism in the future, he or she is more likely to do so amicably.

Prepare Before Criticizing Others

Examining your own faults and attempting to rectify them will give you an appreciation of how difficult and painful change can be. This will increase your patience for your spouse, because you will understand on a visceral level how difficult it is for him or her to improve. It is important to stay confident and hopeful about your own and your spouse's ability to change for the better. Only then will you have the clarity, equanimity, and energy to forge ahead.

One indicator that you have not yet performed sufficient introspection is that when you discuss some highly-charged issue with your spouse, your manner is abrasive or uncontrolled. It may be tempting to criticize your spouse harshly. For instance, you may want to do so as a means of paying him or her back for all the times he or she disappointed or disparaged you.

But before you rebuke your partner, examine your motives. Do so constructively. Be honest but compassionate with yourself. Be sure that your words are not coming from a desire to criticize or from some inner insecurity. Your sole intent should be to help your spouse and your marriage.

Give Hope Along With Help

The *Frierdiker* Rebbe teaches, "*Chassidic* doctrine demands that before reproving someone else a person must 'pare his own fingernails' in order not to gash the other."[42] In a letter to a zealous pietist, the Rebbe Rayatz advised that when relating to his fellow Jews, he should moderate his biting criticisms and keep them dispassionate—just as a physician, before embarking on any kind of surgical intervention,

---

42 After a person's nails are pared, he must wash his hands. While this can be understood and accepted simply on the physical plane, *Chassidus* explains that symbolically, this indicates the drawing down of intellect into emotion. Water alludes to the intellect and hands symbolize the emotions. A person "paring his nails"—that is, offering criticism—must "wash his hands"—that is, diminish the emotional pain that his criticism might cause by cooling it off with the intellect. This is because, when emotions are aroused to the point of excess, they need to be calmed by the mind (see *Toras Menachem –Hisvaaduyos* 5716 [1956], Vol 1, p 221.) Rabbi Menachem Mendel Schneerson, *Hayom Yom, from Day to Day:* Bi-Lingual Hebrew/English Edition, translated, elucidated, and annotated by Uri Kaploun and Eliyahu Touger (New York: Kehot Publication Society, 2005), 22 Elul, p. 89.

anesthetizes the area to be treated in order to minimize the pain.[43]

When you do take action to point out to your spouse what is bothering you about a specific behavior, make sure to discuss it in a way that leaves him or her feeling hopeful as well. In the long run, this will help you have greater success in accomplishing your goals.

In order to increase the likelihood that your spouse will be receptive to your words, first do a kindness for him or her, in keeping with the advice of the Baal Shem Tov.

For example, let's say a man treats his staff at work with disdain and never considers their personal needs or feelings, as a result of which he has chronic difficulties managing them. His wife believes it would be beneficial for him to be made aware of this shortcoming. She may begin by providing him with some tangible benefit.

By personally performing a kindness for him, the wife demonstrates in an obvious way that she cares about her husband. Once he realizes that she has his best interests at heart, he will likely be more open to what she has to say. "Without an immediate and believable demonstration of her concern, however, her advice is likely to sound patronizing or appear to be a cheap substitute for real help."[44]

---

43 See his *Igros Kodesh* (New York: Kehot Publication Society, 1993) letter #610, Vol. 2, pp. 475-476.

44 *Mystery of Marriage*, p. 148

Self Esteem is Critical

It is important to realize that being overly critical is often a sign that one is suffering from a diminished sense of self-worth. If you think that this is true of yourself or your spouse, do your utmost to boost your own or your spouse's self-esteem.

According to Rabbi Yitzchak Ginsburgh, a cure for poor self-esteem is to realign one's consciousness with one's Divine soul. Learning Torah provides the essential spiritual nourishment that reconnects a person's soul to its Divine source.

The breath of our words when we are praying or learning Torah brings a level of the Garden of Eden down around us. Our voices raised in prayer and learning connect us to G-d. It is stated in *Asarah Ma'amarot*[45] that the atmosphere envelopes every individual, and in this atmosphere are recorded all his good thoughts and utterances of Torah and divine worship. Torah is a conduit for G-d's breath, which comes down as powerful energy which can melt away our negativity. Learning Torah out loud is our way of exchanging breath with Hashem; it is almost like a kiss, when the breath of each partner is infused into the other.

---

45   Rabbi Menahem Azariah da Fano (also called Immanuel da Fano, and Rema MiPano) 1548-1620, an Italian rabbi, Talmudist, and Kabbalist, *Sefer Asarah Ma'amarot* (Jerusalem: Mechon Yismach Lev - Torat Moshe, 2000).

The Lubavitcher Rebbe recommends that spouses learn together regularly[46]: "It is also very desirable that [husband and wife] should have at least one regular shiur (study period) in a section of Torah which is of interest to both, such as on the weekly Sedra (Torah portion), or on a timely subject connected with a particular season or festival."

When spouses learn Torah with each other, they connect with the *Shechinah*, and they connect with each other as well. As breath is exchanged through our holy words, the two souls meld, and what is missing from one partner is supplied by the other. Through properly applied speech, one person's good qualities can infuse into another.

Speaking Kindly

When you verbalize your emotions, they grow in intensity. On the other hand, when you refrain from verbalizing them, they dissipate until they vanish entirely.

Speaking angrily fuels a person's anger and may lead to outbursts of rage. Conversely, when a person speaks words of love, his affectionate feelings are intensified,[47] for the act of verbalizing draws his attention to all of the wonderful qualities of the object of his love.

As you express loving feelings toward your spouse he or she will feel a natural desire to reciprocate. The more honor

46 *Letters from the Rebbe*, p. 192.
47 Ibid.

and affection you show your spouse, the more he or she is likely to respond in kind.

Expending the effort to offer praise and admiration instead of frequent criticism can really change your spouse for the better, because praising someone for a particular attribute actually elicits that attribute.[48] Consistently praising your spouse's positive attributes reinforces those attributes, as he or she begins to live up to that image of him or herself.

Kindness of Giving

When a husband and wife give to each other in a spirit of kindness, they maximize the love between themselves.

Rabbi Moshe Hecht related in a *devar Torah* (a Torah lecture) that of the 10 faculties of the human soul,[49] there is none called *ahava*, "love." There is, however, one called *chesed*, "kindness." The root of the Hebrew word *ahava* is *hav*, "to give." This indicates that intrinsically there is no such thing as love. Rather, love is a spillover of the faculty of kindness, which is expressed in giving.

Giving is thus the essence of love.

When one gives to another person, feelings of love for that person increase. When a person stops giving to

48 *Derech Mitzvosecha Shoresh Mitzvos HaTefila*, chap 9, page 118.

49 Please see Appendix for an elucidation of these faculties.

someone whom he loves, his feelings of love tends to diminish. Therefore, in order to strengthen your love for your spouse, you should look for more ways of giving to him or her.

Rabbi Hecht illustrated this point as follows: At the beginning of *Parshas Terumah*, we are taught that Hashem did not tell the Jews what specific amounts of material to donate for the building of the *mishkan*, the Tabernacle. Instead, He said that they should offer as much as their hearts desired.

The intended lesson for all times is that we should give from our hearts, both in our service of Hashem and in our relationships with other people. In so doing, we emulate the giving nature of Hashem.

Rabbi Hecht then told the following story:

A young woman named Sarah graduated from medical school. She thought that she would go to a prestigious hospital for her internship but instead was sent to a makeshift clinic in a Spanish-speaking town. One day a Hispanic girl came into the emergency room, bleeding profusely. Her hand had been severed. She needed a blood transfusion so urgently that there was no time to do a blood test. The girl was asked if she had any relatives and she replied that she had a younger brother, who was nearby.

Sarah thought that the brother's blood would be the best option under the circumstances, and so she sent someone to fetch him. When he came in, she told him in pidgin Spanish that his sister's life was in danger and that without his blood she would die.

The boy agreed to give his blood. After the transfusion was already in progress, he asked Sarah how soon he himself would die. She was taken aback until she realized that he thought that by giving his sister his blood he would lose his life—yet he was willing to make that sacrifice for her sake.

That was true giving. That was true love.

Beneficial Kindness

When you interact with your spouse in a kind way, you will gain all of the benefits associated with performing *mitzvos*. You will grow less defensive and find it easier to let go of your resentments. Your compassion and your ability to express tenderness will increase, as will the positive energy between you and your spouse.

As you make the connection between the kind deeds that you perform for your spouse and the spiritual meaning of those acts, you will grow happier and more loving, and that will have a beneficial impact on your marriage.

Exercises/Meditations

Practice acts of kindness toward your spouse. Try to predict his or her needs before he or she expresses them. For example, if your spouse likes a cup of tea or coffee in the morning, try to have one ready when he or she wakes up. Offer it with a smile and a pleasant "Good morning." Or, if your spouse is entering the house laden with packages, stop what you are doing to help. As you do so, greet your spouse pleasantly and with a smile.

If you can afford it, get household help. The Lubavitcher Rebbe was once asked if folding one's *tallis* (prayer shawl) right after Shabbos is a *segulah* (a good omen) for *shalom bayis*. The Rebbe replied that helping clean the dishes is a better *segulah*.

Compliment your spouse often, even for small and ordinary acts. When you offer such a compliment, smile warmly and speak lovingly, even if that means exaggerating. The Talmud (*Kesuvos* 111b) tells us, "It is better to show your white teeth to your friend than to serve him milk." That is, a smile and words of encouragement often benefit a person more than material assistance can.

Visualize yourself in a situation to which you usually respond with anger or impatience, and with a frown or scowl upon your face. Now visualize yourself responding with a smile and kind words.

Practice a pleasant expression in front of a mirror until you become used to it. Visualize yourself maintaining this pleasant expression throughout various interactions with your spouse.

To inspire yourself to act kindly toward your spouse, consider that although Achitofel taught King David only two things[50], King David remained so grateful that even after Achitofel turned against him he accorded him great respect, referring to him as his teacher, guide, and intimate.[51] Focus on two occasions on which your spouse has done a beneficial action for you. Perhaps he or she assisted you with some difficult chore (albeit with some negative comments), gave you an unexpected compliment, or even surprised you with a small but thoughtful gift. Perhaps he or she simply did not do a negative action when you were expecting one. For these reasons alone, you can thank your spouse sincerely and praise him or her for the effort (or the restraint).

Establish a regular time of Torah study for yourself, and encourage your spouse to do so as well. Be sure only to encourage and not to pressure.

Establish a regular period of Torah study for you and your spouse together.

---

50 Achitofel taught King David: 1) to study Torah with a partner, for only then would the learning endure, and 2) to run to prayer like a person following the king. *Kallah Rabbasi* 8.

51 See *Rashi* on *Pirkei Avos* 6:2.

Say "I love you" to your spouse, often. Even though at first doing so may feel forced, eventually you will find that your feelings match your words.

Points for Practical Reflection

- The way you act influences the way you are.

- Acting kind leads to being kind.

- A pleasant expression leads to a pleasant disposition.

- Smiles given usually result in smiles returned.

- Verbalizing emotions intensifies the emotion.

- Speaking kindly leads to feeling kind. Speaking lovingly leads to feelings of love.

- Being nice to your spouse increases your compassion, which increases the positive energy in your marriage.

- Acting kindly to your spouse is a mitzvah and thus confers tremendous spiritual benefits on you.

- Rebuke ought to be motivated by the true desire to help your spouse or your efforts will be dismissed simply as criticism.

- Providing some tangible benefit to your partner before offering criticism renders the rebuke more acceptable.

- Offering criticism calmly and patiently mitigates its sting.

- Excessive criticism may spring from low self-esteem.

- Learning Torah is a cure for low self-esteem.

- Learning Torah connects your soul to G-d.

- Learning Torah with your spouse connects your two souls together.

5
—

Working From The Inside Out—You Think, You Can

Once we have begun to work on our physical behavior, the next step is to work on our mental behavior. According to the Alter Rebbe, there is no question that we have the ability to control and direct our thoughts. He teaches that[52]:

Man was so created from birth, that every person may, with the power of the will in his brain—i.e., the will created of his mind's understanding—restrain himself and control the drive of his heart's lust, preventing his heart's desires from finding expression in deed, word, and thought, and [he can, if his

---

52 *Likkutei Amarim*, vol 1, chap. 12, pages 176-177.

mind wills it,] divert his attention completely from that which his heart craves [and turn his attention] to the exact opposite direction.

Distressed by his immature behavior and his seemingly arrogant dreams, the sons of Yaakov throw their brother Yosef (Joseph) into a pit that (Gen. 37:24) "was empty, there was no water in it." Rashi comments on this verse that the pit was dry, but filled with snakes and scorpions. The Rebbe[53] uses this verse to stress our ability and responsibility to control our thoughts: the Torah is compared to water, and if one's mind and heart are empty of the water of Torah, they will instead be filled with the "snakes and scorpions" of negativity, aimlessness, evil thoughts, and depression.

Although the most powerful motivation for change is a desire to attain holiness, mundane purposes will also work. Thus, the Alter Rebbe teaches that "the principle of mind over heart holds true even where self-restraint is dictated by simple logic rather than by a desire to achieve a state of holiness."[54]

This phenomenon is readily apparent in our everyday lives. For instance, a man leaves home upset. It's one of those mornings when everything has gone wrong. Still angry, he arrives late to his office, where his boss reprimands him. Although just a short while ago he lost his temper with his wife and children, now his mind counsels him:

53 *Likkutei Sichot: Vayechi.*

54 *Tanya*, chap. 12, pp. 176-7.

"You can't afford to lose your cool now, or you'll get fired. Swallow your pride and just say you're sorry!"

And so he restrains his anger, just as one steps on the brakes of a car to slow it down.

Bridge Between Heart and Head

In this regard, the Frierdiker Rebbe relates[55] that his father, the Rebbe Rashab, once had to consult a physician. When the physician asked about his schedule, the Rebbe replied that he spent much time learning Torah (specifically, *Chassidus*).

When the doctor then asked about the nature of this study, the Rebbe Rashab replied, "The discipline of *Chassidus* requires that the head explain to the heart what the person should want, and [that] the heart... implement in the person's life that which the head understands."

"How can this be done?" the doctor asked. "Are head and heart not two continents separated by a vast ocean?"

The Rebbe Rashab answered, "The task is to build a bridge that will span these two 'continents,' or at least connect them with a wire much like telephone lines and electrical wires, so that the light of the head should reach the heart."

---

55 *Likkutei Dibburim*, vol. 1, pg. 82.

It will be much easier for your mind to affect your character when you fill your mind with holiness and G-d's wisdom, which you do when you learn Torah.

Tefillah Changes Your Animal Soul—and Your Brain

Through Torah learning, one comes to a realization of Hashem's wisdom and greatness. However, as the Rebbe Rashab teaches in *Kuntres HaTefilah*, many people learn Torah but do not change their character traits. What does work to change one's *middos* is meditative prayer, when one concentrates with deep contemplation on the words of the *tefillos* and their meanings, and on Hashem's wisdom and greatness in conjunction with prayer. Through meditative prayer, one draws Hashem's light into his or her mind and changes the actual physical structure of the brain.

In 2005, Sara Lazar, Ph.D., a molecular biologist at Harvard, conducted a groundbreaking study that showed that the cortex of the brain (the area thought to be involved in integrating emotional and cognitive processes) became thicker in research subjects who meditated regularly. The study also showed that meditation may reduce the thinning of the cortex typically associated with aging.[56]

---

56 Sara W Lazar, Catherine E Kerr, Rachel H Wasserman, et al "Meditation experience is associated with increased cortical thickness" *Neuroreport*,16(17):1893–1897 (Nov 28, 2005). Aging and pathology are possible

Two years later, Dr. Lazar conducted another study at the Massachusetts General Hospital, which corroborated her original findings. Her research also showed that those people who meditated regularly possessed greater mastery over their emotions and experienced a lower susceptibility to illnesses of the mind, especially those associated with aging, such as dementia, Parkinson's disease, and Alzheimer's disease.[57]

If secular meditation can effect such positive changes in the brain, then certainly infusing our mind with holy thoughts will change our brain structure for the better, resulting in improvements in our emotions and actions.[58]

By analogy, with the invention of the laser and the discovery of its many applications in medicine, we now have a greater appreciation of the power of light than ever before. Today, laser beams are used for a variety of medical purposes, from cleaning teeth to treating cancer. If ordinary

---

sources of cortical thinning, and Dr. Lazar's study showed that "regular meditation practice may slow age-related thinning of the frontal cortex."

57   According to Dr. Lazar, "The gray matter comprises the thinking and computing cells of the brain, while the white matter is primarily the wires connecting them. So we are looking at how much gray matter there is in the participants' brains, which reflects how much computing power they have." The implication is that the more gray matter exists, the better. For example, studies have shown that people who speak two languages have a thicker cortex in the language areas of the brain than people who speak only one language. "It appears that when you acquire new knowledge, new areas grow," she notes. Interview with David Van Nuys, PhD "Neuroscience of Meditation" (Dec. 3, 2009).

58   Based on a discourse of the Lubavitcher Rebbe. See Rabbi Majeski's *The Chassidic Approach to Joy.*

light can heal the body, how much more can G-d's holy light from the Torah heal a person's mind?[59]

In With the Good

When you intensively learn Torah, you change the way you think, which in turn affects your attitudes, perceptions, speech and actions.

Thus, learning Torah should be one of the first steps that you take to control your thoughts and actions. Changing intellectual awareness, the Alter Rebbe teaches, is easier to accomplish than directly changing character traits, because our intellect is less subject to evil influences than our emotions are.[60] Rabbi Laibl Wolf points out, when discussing meditation, that in physiological terms our emotional response is triggered three to four times more quickly than our intellectual response to a stimulus.[61] That is, it is easier to train our rational self—which will respond more appropriately to a tense situation, than to train ourselves to slow down our emotional reactions.

The responsibility to learn Torah rests equally upon men and women. The Lubavitcher Rebbe teaches that in

---

59 Rebbe Rashab, *Kuntres Hatefilla.*

60 Our emotional soul is closer to *klipah* than our intellectual soul is, therefore it is more affected by it. Please see Appendix for a more in-depth explanation of this point.

61 Heard by author in one of Rabbi Wolf's classes on meditation.

our times, when women often work outside the home and consequently are more exposed to secular influences, "if the policy of not teaching Torah at an advanced level is upheld, the result will be that a girl's sophisticated worldly knowledge—which is likely to harbor many ideas that are antithetical to Torah—will be insubstantially compensated for by her rudimentary Torah knowledge."[62]

The Lubavitcher Rebbe states that the woman's Torah learning brings the warmth of *Yiddishkeit* (Jewish life) to her family. Because women are typically more nurturing and adept at motivating children than men are, a knowledgeable woman often possesses a superior ability to inspire her family to perform *mitzvos* with enthusiasm.[63]

Spiritual Power of Love

Learning Torah leads one to a closer relationship with G-d, which develops into a more intense connection and love for Him. The Alter Rebbe teaches that each of us already possesses this great love for Hashem, which He bestowed upon us as a gift—or, more accurately, as an inheritance—in the merit of our Patriarchs.[64] This dormant love, which needs only to be aroused, is so powerful that when we do

---

62 Based on *Sichos Kodesh* 5741 vol 2, p. 809ff; *Sichas Shabbos Emor* 5750.

63 *Sichos in English, Adar II-Iyar 5744*, vol. 20, pp. 24-30.

64 *Lessons in Tanya*, p. 249.

bring it to our awareness it has the ability to steer us away from negative thoughts, words, and deeds.

Even the average person can be inspired to overcome his temptations by the knowledge that he has great spiritual power. However, when you are in the midst of a heated moment, such as an argument, you may find it difficult to draw upon this awareness.

It is thus best to accustom yourself to access this hidden love, with its attendant reservoir of strength, when you are calm. A good way to do this is to put yourself into this state of awareness every time you pray. For instance, when you recite passages in the prayers that mention Avraham, Yitzchak, and Yaakov, you can recall that in their merit we have received the ability to love Hashem. Then, when you are familiar with this state of mind, you can more easily achieve it even at turbulent moments.

Positive Outlook, Positive Outcome

When we control our thoughts and emotions, we can change the way we think of ourselves and of others. We can choose to focus on seeing the people and events in our lives in a positive light. Because what a person thinks affects every aspect of how he or she functions, this positive outlook leads to positive outcomes.[65]

When you work on purifying your thoughts about people, you improve the way that they will behave toward you and you increase their readiness to live up to your positive expectations of them.

Thus, our Sages teach (*Pirkei Avos* 1:12) that Aharon HaKohen (Aaron the High Priest) drew others closer to Torah by praising them—even with white lies—and giving them unconditional acceptance and love. They started telling themselves, "If Aharon HaKohen believes in me and treats me like royalty, then I must be worthy." That motivated them to live up to his high opinion of them.[66]

Negative Thinking Hurts

Similarly, harboring negative thoughts leads to negative consequences. The Alter Rebbe teaches that the sudden appearance in a person's mind of a negative thought is not under his control and thus is not his fault. That is, one is not responsible for any negative thoughts about one's spouse that come spontaneously to mind. But one *is* responsible

---

65 Numerous scientific studies offer evidence of the power of positive imagery to boost the immune system, alleviate pain, and promote faster healing after surgery, among other beneficial effects. Please see Appendix for more on this topic.

66 *Tractate Kallah Rabasi* 3:1.

for what one does with that negative thought once it has entered the mind.

One is also responsible, to a large extent, for the frequency with which these negative thoughts arise. The more negative one's outlook, the more receptive one is to negative thoughts. A negative mindset will, so to speak, invite negative thoughts to enter, just as a person tends to associate with others of similar interests.

Negative thinking harms a person spiritually as well as physically. Someone who thinks or behaves negatively toward their partner is succumbing to the wiles of the evil inclination, and as such is affecting himself negatively as well, for *Chassidus* teaches that the garments of one's soul become "stained" when one indulges in negative thoughts, words, or deeds, thereby erecting a barrier between oneself and Hashem.[67] We are all expected to do our utmost to banish such thinking before it takes hold and influences our behavior.

The Alter Rebbe writes[68]:

Therefore, my beloved and dear ones, I beg again and again that each of you exert himself with all of his heart and soul to firmly implant in his heart a love for his fellow Jew, and in the words of Scripture [Zecharia 8:1], "Let none of you consider in your heart what is evil for his fellow." Moreover, [such a consideration] should never arise in one's heart [in the first place]; and if it does arise... one should push it away from

67   See *Tanya*, Chapter 11.

68   *Tanya Iggeres HaKodesh*, Vol 5, chap 22, pages 42-43.

his heart "as smoke is driven away," as if it were an idolatrous thought. For to speak evil [of another] is as grave as idolatry and incest and bloodshed.[69] *And if this be so for speech, [then surely thinking evil about another is even worse]; for all the wise of heart are aware of the greater impact [on the soul] of thought over speech, whether for the good or for the better.*

In one of his classes on the subject of angels,[70] Rabbi Laibl Wolf provides a kabbalistic perspective on how our thoughts affect our relationships. He teaches that according to the *kabbalah,* our positive thoughts about a person create "good angels" and our negative thoughts create "bad angels." These angels then hover around us.

When you meet a person about whom you had a negative thought, the bad angel that you created interacts with that person's angels (created by his own deeds) and repels them. In more down-to-earth terms, that person senses your negative "vibes" about him.

As soon as you do *teshuvah* (repent) for having had that unkind thought, the negative angel melts away, and the barrier between you and that person falls away.

The same applies to your marriage. Developing a more positive attitude toward your spouse will help make your relationship healthy. As you engage in some honest soul-searching and examine your true judgments and feelings about your spouse, you will more clearly see where you can improve your thoughts about him or her.

69 *Arachin* 15b.

70 Rabbi Laibl Wolf, *Dream Angel* CD.

Be Magical

One day, while trying to contact the washing machine repairman, I was placed on hold and a song came on the line that went something like, "Everything she does is magical." As I waited for a seemingly interminable amount of time, I remembered the *Chassidic* teaching that everything we hear and see imparts a lesson, so I tried to figure out what lesson I was supposed to derive from this song.

Then I remembered a teaching from *Tanya* to the effect that good thoughts, speech and actions elevate a person's soul, making him or her more "magical," or wondrous, in Hashem's eyes.

Now, every time I heard the word "magical" repeated, I was overcome by a desire to be more magical in G-d's eyes. And I came to realize that being "magical" in G-d's eyes means being more "magical" with people, especially those closest to me. I reflected that when I am careful to demonstrate how precious my relationships are to me, they come alive and become magical. This requires more than mere lip service. My speech and deeds should consistently express love and caring.

Love Yourself, Love Others

The Torah commands us to "love your fellow as yourself" (*Vayikra* 19:18). But how can a mandated love equal a person's natural feelings for himself? And what if we do not love ourselves? When a person lacks a healthy self-love and dislikes himself because of his flaws, he has difficulty loving others, since they too possess flaws.

The answer is, as the Alter Rebbe teaches, that just as each Jew possesses an instinctual love for Hashem, so each Jew possesses a natural instinct to love himself and his fellow Jew. Thus, in Rabbi Yosef Wineberg's words, "one Jew need not create a love for another. The love is an inborn characteristic of his soul, on account of its root in G-dliness which is common to all souls; it is as natural as the love between brothers."[71] The commandment to "love your fellow as yourself" merely directs us to activate our hidden, natural capacity.

The more that a person works to manifest his G-dly essence and refine himself, the more is he attuned to his soul, and the easier it is for him to access this natural instinct to love his fellow Jew.

Conversely, the more that a person indulges his materialistic aspects or remains with unrefined or unhealthy characteristics, the farther he is removed from his soul, and the more removed from being able to love his fellow Jew.

It is crucial that we protect ourselves from allowing our own negative behaviors and attitudes, and those of the others in our lives, to bury this natural, instinctual love. It is true that even after a person has achieved a healthy self-love and self-confidence, loving others can pose a

71 Wineberg, *Lessons in Tanya* Vol.1, *Likkutei Amarim*, Chap. 32, pp. 421-423.

daunting challenge. But we may be sure that since G-d has commanded us to love our fellow Jew, He has created us with the ability to do so.

Exercises And Meditations

Visualize yourself beginning a new, healthy habit. Imagine this habit being engraved into the grooves of your brain. Then visualize your brain building a "wiring" system that connects it to your heart, until you feel empowered to achieve.

Imagine yourself driving a powerful car which can only be controlled through your thoughts. You know it is imperative to keep the vehicle from exceeding a certain speed in order to avoid a destructive crash or collision. You direct all your mental energy toward keeping the car running smoothly, adjusting your speed and grip to accommodate the twists and turns of the road, always alert to the possibility of unexpected obstacles. You practice mental control of the vehicle every day, until you become its master.

Designate a set time for Torah learning. Optimally, each session should be no less than 15 minutes, but you may begin at five minutes and gradually increase the duration. During this time, focus only on the Torah topic. If you are interrupted, begin again. It is best to read Torah passages out loud, as this reinforces the learning and serves as an aid in focusing.

Visualize the Torah you are learning as beams of light. Visualize these beams focused on a target. Visualize this light cleansing and healing the targeted area. Finally, visualize G-d's holy light entering and healing your heart and mind and banishing the darkness of the animal soul.

Imagine yourself accompanied by the angels created by your thoughts. Realize that you can surround yourself with positive forces of your own making.

Visualize the angels you have created through your thoughts about your spouse. If necessary, visualize your *teshuvah* dissolving the negative angels around you and your spouse.

Imagine that you are standing next to an artist and admiring her work. You are so impressed by her creative abilities that you gush forth words of praise: "Your hands are golden. It is amazing how you blend those colors. The picture looks so real. You're so talented." Imagine what pleasure the artist receives from these words. In the same way, when you appreciate that you yourself are G-d's handiwork, a Divinely created being fulfilling G-d's will in the world, you give G-d—the Artist—the ultimate pleasure. Imagine how much greater His pleasure will be when you appreciate your spouse and your marriage as His handiwork.

Points For Practical Reflection

- We have the ability to control and direct our thoughts.

- Reprogramming habitual responses takes repeated efforts and much time, but perseverance brings about change.

- The desire to attain holiness is the most powerful motivation for change, but mundane purposes will also work.

- Praying and learning Torah should be the first steps that you take to gain self-control.

- Praying and learning Torah increases our own Divine wisdom.

- Meditating on Hashem's wisdom and greatness draws Hashem's light into our mind and changes the actual physical structure of the brain.

- It is easier to change our intellectual awareness than to directly change our character traits.

- A positive outlook leads to a more positive outcome.

- One is not responsible for negative thoughts that come to mind spontaneously, but one is responsible for what is done with those thoughts.

- Negative thoughts create a barrier between you and others.

- *Teshuvah* can break down the barrier of negativity.

- You may not be able to control other people or situations, but you can always work on controlling your attitude.

6

Respect And Humility

Prayer and Torah learning are essential steps to self-improvement and improved relationships in the category of *ben adam lemakom*, "between man and the Creator," and equally important in the category of *ben adam lechaveiro*, "between man and his fellow man," interpersonal relationships.

"*Derech eretz kadmah leTorah*, respect comes before learning."[72] Treating others with respect is a fundamental element of a Torah life. Without this essential character trait, one cannot fully absorb the Torah's teachings. The students of Rabbi Akiva, although all superior Torah

72 *Vayikra Rabbah* chap. 9.

scholars, did not truly respect each other and the different perspectives they brought to their learning; this deficiency had long-ranging negative effects.

Mutual Respect

The respect that a husband and wife ought to show each other possesses a quality beyond that which we are supposed to accord each other as Jews. Although *shalom bayis* will be benefitted by even that general level of respect, it will be immeasurably strengthened if a couple can reach that higher level specific to spouses.

A story is told of Rabbi Aryeh Levin that underscores this point. The accepted custom in Yerushalayim when Rabbi Levin became engaged was that the couple exchange gifts. Neither Rabbi Levin nor his orphaned bride, Tzipporah Channah, had any money. So, instead of gifts, Rabbi Levin suggested that they each promise that throughout their married life, they would "always consider the other's feelings in everything we do. That will be the greatest gift we can give each other, and it will not cost us a single coin."[73]

---

73   Shmuel Himelstein, *Wisdom and Wit* (New York: Mesorah Publishing Ltd., 2003) p. 122.

Reciprocity

The principle of reciprocity is the key to a harmonious relationship. This reciprocity occurs even when one spouse does not reciprocate. As long as one spouse demonstrates acceptance, respect, and love, eventually the other will begin to act in the same fashion. In this way, you contribute toward the creation of an environment where peace and joy can flourish. Ultimately, the more you work on having a humble and positive attitude, the more you will gain.

The verse in *Pirkei Avos* (2:4) perfectly describes this principle of reciprocity: "Treat His will as if it were your own will, so that He will treat your will as if it were His will. Nullify your will before His will, so that He will nullify the will of others before your will." Although this primarily applies to one's relationship to Hashem, it is equally applicable to the marital relationship.

True Appreciation

Sima Basry explains, in her book *The Challenge of Marriage*[74]: "Respect, when given wholeheartedly, and in an encouraging way, has great effects. When respect for one's partner gushes forth, not as superficial flattery, but from a real appreciation of his worth and a realization of the

---

74   Sima Basry, *The Challenge of Marriage: A Guide to Married Life*, translated by Avraham Shulman, (Jerusalem, Hakisav Institute, 1982) page 59.

uniqueness of his soul, then it will be a light which warms up his soul and brings about a blooming of his inner, good self."

Respect and consideration for a spouse's feelings are the basis for a great relationship. Some women may bristle at the idea that they are obligated to honor their husbands in a manner similar to that in which a child should honor his parents (for instance, not to say outright that he made a mistake). We need to remember though that men are similarly obligated to honor their wives.

Benefits of Respect

As Sima Basry points out, it often happens that "[a] family's misfortune begins when its members forget their obligations toward each other while still demanding what they feel is due to them."[75] It follows, however, that when those obligations are met, the demands will become requests and the family's fortunes will turn for the better.

Mrs. Basry explains this phenomenon by clarifying that the respect between spouses is indeed a separate requirement from the respect which ought to be given to everyone else[76]:

75 Basry, page 57.
76 Ibid, pp. 60ff.

"We should realize that a husband and wife together form a new entity, in addition to their separate selves. This new entity requires a special type of respect of its own.

Even if a person is one of the greats of his generation, respect for his partner will give him the completeness and wholeness for which he was created.

This mutual respect brings about an atmosphere of appreciation of each other's value which, in turn, brings about a deep recognition of the power and uniqueness of each other's soul.

This merely stresses the importance of reciprocity, for when we recognize "the power and uniqueness" of our spouse's soul, we really are being shown the power and uniqueness of our own soul.

Judging Favorably Leads to Humility

The way we perceive events and people in our lives is not the only way they can be viewed. Our perspective may differ markedly from that of others, even those who have shared the same experience with us.

An elderly lady, in an airport lounge awaiting her flight, bought a box of cookies and sat down next to a teenage girl. The woman took out a magazine and began to read, when out of the corner of her eye, she noticed that the girl was eating one of her cookies. "How disrespectful young people are today," the woman thought, "taking something without even asking permission." The teenager ate one cookie after another. Fearing that she would not have any cookies left for herself, the elderly lady began eating the cookies as well. As the teenager did not stop taking her cookies, the elderly woman became more and more disgusted and looked at the teenager with disdain. The girl just smiled at her.

At last there was just one cookie left. The woman waited to see what the girl would do. To her amazement, the girl took it—and then broke the cookie in two and offered one half to the woman. That did it! The elderly woman opened her mouth to scold this teenager for her presumption. But just then came the announcement that it was time to board, and the elderly woman opened her purse to get out her boarding pass. Inside, to her shock, was her package of cookies—unopened.

She realized that all along she had been eating the teenager's cookies. Now she felt deeply embarrassed and stupid. She wanted to apologize, but the girl had already left and the woman had no time to search for her, as she had to hurry to catch her plane. She wished that she had not jumped to conclusions and had instead given the teenager the benefit of the doubt.

Since she couldn't apologize to the girl personally, she said to herself, "The least I can do is resolve that I will give others the benefit of the doubt instead of rushing to judgment."

Her mistake taught her such a lesson that from that day forward she was no longer the same person.

Relationships are created moment by moment. Each time we judge others favorably, we steer our relationships in the right direction, as shown in the following episode.

An elementary school teacher had two bad habits. One was that he was often late, and the other was that he was prone to react angrily to his students' provocations.

At the beginning of a new school year, he resolved to work on overcoming these problems: to arrive at school on time and, if he grew angry at a student, to calm down before speaking with the student.

On the first day of school, his alarm clock didn't go off and he arrived late. The next morning, he was at the bus stop on time, but the bus failed to arrive, as a result of which he had to hail a cab, which cost him a pretty penny and dropped him off just as the bell was ringing.

As he burst through the front door and was dashing to his classroom, one of his students from the previous year stopped in front of him and pointed at his watch.

The teacher was furious that this student should publicly embarrass him for being late, and he was about to say something when he remembered his resolution. Instead he simply said, "Excuse me," and hurried up the stairs to his classroom. Later on during recess, that same student approached him and said, "I was happy to see you this morning."

"Why?" the teacher asked coolly.

"I figured that if I saw my favorite teacher at the beginning of the day, I'd have a good year." The boy raised his wrist and displayed his wristwatch. "I wanted to show you the new watch I got from my parents for my birthday."

The teacher felt humbled. Not only had he misread the boy's behavior, but he hadn't even realized that the boy considered him his favorite teacher. Fortunately, by controlling his emotional reaction that morning, he had preserved the goodwill that the student felt toward him and maintained the student's dignity as well as his own.

When you are upset with yourself, or with others, you may feel an immediate sense of gratification if you allow yourself to let off steam. You may feel justified in reacting in such a way to what you consider to be provocation. But more often than not you will afterwards regret the loss of control. You may find that the "provocation" was nothing more than your own misreading of a situation.

Worse still, such outbursts cause much unnecessary tension and stress to all family members, and their cumulative effect is damaging not only to your own self-esteem but to the self-esteem of your spouse and your children.

Don't *Act* Humble, *Be* Humble

Our Sages teach, "Be humble of spirit before every man" (*Pirkei Avos* 4:12). Some commentators interpret this *mishnah* to mean that even if a person considers someone else to be inferior to him he should treat that person with deference. But the Alter Rebbe emphasizes that by stating "*be* humble," rather than "*act* humble," the *mishnah* is telling us that we should feel humble even in the presence of someone whom we consider to be acting improperly.

But why should we be humble before someone like that?

The Alter Rebbe explains[77] that the answer is to be found in the instruction of our Sages, "Do not judge your fellow until you have reached his place" (*Pirkei Avos* 2:5). No man can ever reach another's place; hence a person can never really be qualified to judge someone else. Only G-d, Who is omniscient and omnipresent, can reach a person's true place and judge him.

We need also to consider the "place" of a person, that is, his present state. This "place" encompasses not only his physical environment but his spiritual environment as well, including his innate nature and temperament, and the situations that brought him to this state.

---

77 *Tanya* Vol 1, *Likkutei Amarim*, chap 30, pages 393-394.

Humility Leads to Harmony

Every day we are faced with the temptation to think, speak, and act in destructive ways. Recognizing the incredible power of your thoughts and words will motivate you to fight this urge. Instead, use your thoughts and words to bring more respect, harmony, and unity into your marital relationship.

The Torah stresses that humility is a worthy and virtuous trait which should be cultivated by everyone striving to be righteous. Arrogance, the polar opposite of humility, is considered unworthy. Arrogance can destroy a marriage; humility can save it.

The following story of the wedding of Rebbetzin Devorah Leah, daughter of the Mitteler Rebbe (Rabbi Dovber, 1773-1827, son of the Alter Rebbe, and the second leader of Chabad), teaches an inspirational lesson about humility.[78]

The Mitteler Rebbe's daughter was betrothed to [R. Yaakov Yisrael Twersky,] the son of Reb Mordechai of Chernobyl. During the wedding, when Reb Mordechai asked the Rebbe to present a Torah insight, the Rebbe declined, suggesting that Reb Mordechai himself say something. This is what he said:

"We find that our Matriarch Rivkah covered herself with a veil when she first met her groom, the Patriarch Yitzchak

---

78 Rafael Nachman Kahn, *Extraordinary Chassidic Tales* (New York: Otsar Sifrei Lubavitch, 1997) vol. 3:102.

(Genesis 24:65). Rashi translates: 'vatiskos, *"she veiled herself"*
in the reflexive form, as in vatikover, *"she was buried" (Genesis*
35:8) and vatishover, *"and it was broken" (I Sam. 4:18).*[79]

"*Now, there are three stages in life: birth, marriage and
death. These times always cause a tumult; joyful merriment
when one is born and [when one] marries, mournful
bereavement when one passes away. During birth and death,
the one responsible for all the attention is indifferent to the
commotion he is causing. It is only in marriage when one
appreciates the tumult being generated, and it is probable that
this will bring him to arrogance and make him haughty.*

"*Rivkah, however, was different. Even during her marriage
she veiled herself, exemplifying humility and modesty. She was
indifferent to all the commotion—as if she were being born or
buried.*"

One who attains humility treats their spouse with
respect. Then the spouse feels acknowledged and validated,
and reciprocates in kind. The Alter Rebbe explains the verse
(Proverbs 27:19), "As waters mirror the face to the face, so
does the heart of man to man" to mean that just as water
naturally reflects an image, it is natural for a person to
reflect the emotions directed at him or her by another.

---

79 The phrase "she veiled herself" deals with marriage. The phrase "and she
    was buried" deals with death. And the phrase "and it was broken" refers to
    birth, because the news of Eli's sudden, violent death shocked his pregnant
    daughter-in-law into giving birth.

Humility, Not Humiliation

Our Sages declare, "The path of the righteous is best: They are humiliated, but they do not humiliate in return; they hear themselves insulted, but they do not retort; they act out of love, and are happy even in their affliction."[80] Three distinct categories are mentioned here, in ascending order: "Those who are humiliated, but do not humiliate in return" do respond to the insults of others, but do not retaliate in kind. Those of the second category "hear themselves insulted but do not retort" at all. Those of the third category actually "are happy in affliction"—because they remember their past sins, and are glad to accept their present suffering as a means of penance, or as a way by which to show their faith and pass their test.

Therefore, on those occasions that you feel that you have been hurt or insulted by your spouse, set aside your pain and focus on serving G-d. Utilize your talents to the greatest extent possible. This will help you move forward with your life in a way that will have a beneficial impact on yourself, on your spouse, and on the entire cosmos.

G-dly Goal

Marriage is a partnership in which each spouse has a specific, G-d-given role to play. It should never be reduced

---

80   *Tanya, Iggeret HaTeshuva*, Chapter 11.

to a power struggle. Men and women should utilize the particular strengths of their masculine and feminine nature to improve their marriages. The goal should be to build a lasting and peaceful Jewish home, one that is a dwelling place for the *Shechinah*. Those who make this goal their priority will ultimately benefit not only themselves but all their future generations.

Exercises And Meditations

Imagine that you possess a rare and precious artifact, made even more valuable by certain irregularities in its finish. These imperfections may be very small but they enhance immeasurably the total worth of the object. Realizing that, you can ignore those imperfections in your regard for the object. You can even develop an appreciation for those very irregularities and the singular value they add.

Now, regard your spouse as a rare and precious commodity, made even more valuable by certain singularities of character.

Realize that you have willingly accepted the mission of caring for this precious object. You have the power and the ability to keep this object in good shape and even to increase its value. You also have the capability of destroying it.

Reflect on the fact that if you take proper care of this valuable item, your own value will increase, and in the end its original owner will reward you handsomely; if you destroy it, your own value will correspondingly decrease, and you will have to account for your mishandling of the task.

Visualize your spouse as a member of a royal family who is in exile and unaware of his or her true identity. Consider the great opportunity you have to serve this exalted personage, and how greatly your efforts will be appreciated by him/her and the entire royal family later on, when they are ultimately reunited. Think of how much more you would be willing to do for such a person and how humble you would feel around them in their proper environment.

Realize that as a Jew, the descendent of Abraham, you are able to attain humility, no matter how caught up in arrogance you might be. Gain inspiration from the examples of the self-sacrifice of our Patriarchs and Matriarchs.

Points For Practical Reflection

- Replacing arrogance with humility allows you to treat your spouse respectfully.

- Reciprocity is the key to a harmonious relationship.

- When you give your spouse respect, you elevate your own soul.

- When you strive to make your spouse happy, your spouse will strive to make you happy.

- Judging favorably can prevent unpleasant misunderstandings.

- When you judge others, consider all the factors that have gone into their situation and behavior.

- Behavior you consider to be provocative may actually be only your misinterpretation of the situation.

- Marriage is a partnership and each partner has a distinct role.

7

—

The Role of Women

The dynamic in which one respects and helps one's spouse and as a result is elevated as well, is particularly germane to women, as we see from the following teaching of the Lubavitcher Rebbe.[81]

The verse describing Miriam as a prophet identifies her only as the sister of Aharon and not as the sister of Moshe, who was the leader of all Israel and their greatest prophet. Rashi explains that although the omission of Moshe's name might appear to disparage him, the verse is written this way to teach that Miriam was a prophet even before Moshe was born.

81 *Divrei HaMaschil, "Vatikach Miriam HaNeviah."*

According to the Lubavitcher Rebbe,[82] however, telling us that Miriam was a prophet even before Moshe was born does not warrant a phraseology that might be interpreted as implying disrespect for Moshe. Therefore, when the Torah describes Miriam (Exodus 15:20) only as "the sister of Aharon," it must be teaching something more.

The Rebbe goes on to explain that the verse is teaching that even before Moshe was born, Miriam, although she was the eldest child, deferred to her brother Aharon and showed him the utmost respect. This had three results. First, Aharon's spiritual qualities grew. Second, Miriam attained the same good qualities that Aharon was noted for: she too became a pursuer of peace. And third, Miriam's latent abilities developed as well.

Light of Their Life

The Lubavitcher Rebbe applies this to the role of a wife. Women excel at kindness. Therefore, they should infuse their actions with an extra dimension of generosity. A woman should express love for her husband even when he is acting far from lovable.

In one of his discourses,[83] the Lubavitcher Rebbe teaches that women light the *Shabbos* candles because this alludes to their ability to elicit the light of the positive

---

82   See *Likkutei Sichos* vol. 11 pg. 55 and on

83   *Likkutei Sichos*, vol. 9 pg. X and on.

qualities of other people.[84] Women accomplish this by showing love, patience and care. In addition, they do so by serving as a positive example. As the *Frierdiker Rebbe* teaches, "Where the lantern is placed, those who seek light gather around, for light attracts."[85]

Women have the capacity to be this light to their families by putting on a happy face even when they are having marital difficulties. A woman in such a situation may question her need or her ability to do so, but a downcast look serves only to push her spouse further away from her (even though—or because—he himself may be largely responsible for her discontent and sadness).

Women and Humility

Women in particular should strive to cultivate the trait of humility before G-d, emulating our matriarchs Sarah, Rivkah, Rochel, and Leah. The greater a woman's humility, the more she enables her loved ones to flourish and achieve their true potential. The Torah tells us (Genesis 24:64) that Rivkah first saw Yitzchak as he stood praying in a field. Awed by his evident holiness and purity, she fell off her camel, as though bowing to him. By doing so, the Zohar explains, she "subdued the evil force" around

---

84 It is important to note, however, that unmarried men who live alone are also required to light *Shabbos* candles.

85 *Hayom Yom*- 13 Teves.

her.[86] Homiletically, it can be understood to mean that she humbled herself before him, knowingly and willingly.

In her merit, Jewish women have a special ability to subordinate themselves to others—in particular, to their husbands—without their ego being threatened.

Effective Respect

Our sages taught that "a wife shall honor her husband exceedingly."[87] When a wife honors her husband and respects him, she creates an environment that facilitates the actualization of his potential for spiritual greatness. In doing so, she herself grows more elevated and is granted some of the same strengths that her husband possesses. This creates a "holy cycle" of growth.

Many benefits accrue to a couple when a woman acts with humility, generosity, and kindness. For instance, the way in which a wife speaks to her spouse can create a new will within him, as the Lubavitcher Rebbe explains in one of his *sichos*[88]:

…When the husband is, G-d forbid, stumbling, and additionally due to his lack of knowledge, things appear to

---

86 Ginsburgh.

87 Rambam, *Yad Hachazaka, Ishut* 15:19–20.

88 See *Sichos: Acharon Shel Pesach 5730 seif 8. 2nd Day Shvuos 5731 seif 3. 15th Shvat 5732 seif 4.*

him to be the opposite of what they are.... then, in a pleasant
and peaceful manner the wife must "create" his will.... The
"righteous woman" finds pleasant and peaceful ways to create
within her husband a desire to do as the Torah wants.

Similarly, Rabbi Ginsburgh writes[89] that the Chassidic interpretation of the statement (*Tana d'vei Eliahu Rabba* 9), "Who is a proper wife? She who performs [*osah*] the will of her husband," is that she "rectifies" it, explaining: "The most literal reading of *osah* is 'to make,' implying that the proper wife not only 'rectifies' her husband's will but actually 'produces it.'

Contemporary Stress Affects Humility

Today, many women seem to feel that they are being mistreated if they are not pampered by their husbands and if they stay in marriages that do not match their expectations. (This is not meant to imply that there are not cases of genuine abuse in marriage; there are, and they require immediate intervention to ensure the safety of the spouse who is being victimized). There are many cases in which a wife harbors unrealistic expectations of her husband and is ready to jettison a marriage that could be rescued if she was committed to self-improvement and improvement of the relationship.

89   Page 24, fn 50.

The material conditions of previous generations were much more difficult than our own. Yet the women of those generations made great sacrifices. These women evidently found great satisfaction in caring for their families.

We can only speculate as to the reason for the change in attitude today. Perhaps it is due to the different kinds of stress and pressure that modern women experience, or to the greater exposure to secular media. It may be due in part to the fact that women today commonly live far away from their extended families, and as a result they lack the support system that most women in previous generations enjoyed. With fewer family members on whom to rely, a woman can be more prone to tension and anxiety.

Women's Devotion

Today more than ever, it is essential that women realize that they have a special role to play in maintaining a healthy and loving marital relationship.

First, the very fact that a woman is married expresses her devotion, appreciation and commitment to her husband. The *Zohar* teaches that although a man may have to be reincarnated to rectify his sins, that is not the case for a woman, for she accomplishes her rectification in the higher worlds.

However, when a man returns to earth to rectify his sins, his soulmate often cannot bear to be separated from him and so she chooses to return to this world to serve as his helpmate. She thus demonstrates an extraordinary degree of love and devotion.

Since we learn that, in these generations, most people have "old" souls that have undergone previous incarnations, we can assume that most women have chosen to come down to earth to help their soulmates fulfill their spiritual potential. G-d willing, this time around, they will succeed in elevating their husband's soul sufficiently that they can be reunited again eternally.

Optimally, a woman achieves the elevation of her husband's soul through her gentleness, selflessness, love and affection. As Rabbi Ginsburgh writes, "She does this by deepening her faith in G-d and His providence, and her awareness of His purpose in Creation (which entails the rectified image of her husband and their marriage)."[90]

The "rectified image of her husband" refers to the transformation of a man's selfish and unrefined qualities into holy and noble ones. That process is facilitated when a man's wife serves as a positive role model and helpmate. The rectification will also be apparent in the husband's attitude toward his wife: when a wife becomes her husband's greatest supporter and encourages him to succeed in life, he is likely to respond by treating her as his equal or even as his superior.

90 Ibid., page 105.

Women's Spiritual Capacity

In general, women find it easier to improve themselves and others than do men. This is due to two reasons. First, the Almighty granted greater intuition to women than He did to men (see *Niddah* 45b).

Second, as noted earlier in this chapter, He gave women a greater capacity to bring out the spiritual light that lies within themselves and within others.

The Oral Torah itself is an expression of this feminine capacity. The Alter Rebbe states that the verse (Proverbs 1:8), *"You shall not cast off the teaching of your mother,"* refers to the Oral Torah, *"just as all the organs of a child are comprised, very latently, in the sperm of the father, and the mother brings this out into a state of manifestation when giving birth to a child complete with 248 organs and 365 sinews"*[91] (correlating to the number of positive and negative commandments, respectively). That is, as a woman is able to develop the physicality of another human being, she is capable of developing their spirituality as well.

Rabbi Wineberg elucidates that "this is an instance of the 'superior measure of *Binah* [understanding] that was granted to woman,' which is the power to make latent gifts manifest and corporeal."[92]

---

91 *Tanya, Iggeres Hakodesh*, Epistle 29, p. 225.

92 *Tanya, Iggeres Hakodesh*, ibid.

The Lubavitcher Rebbe points out another difference between men and women. Men need to be commanded to perform time-bound *mitzvos*, such as prayer and Torah study, because performing these *mitzvos* is not in their nature. Women do not need to be commanded to perform these *mitzvos* because they naturally possess the desire to do them.[93]

Woman is the "Foundation of the Home"

The Talmud teaches (*Kiddushin* 2b) that "the nature of man is to be influenced by the woman," and that "the Divine Presence does not rest with a man who lives without a wife" (*Yevamos* 62b). Thus, a man is dependent on his wife in order to have G-d's Presence rest upon him and his household.

The *Midrash Rabbah (Bereishis* 17:12) tells us about wicked men who were transformed for the better by righteous wives (and conversely, about righteous men who were influenced toward evil by their wicked wives), and it has been my experience in more than twenty-five years of working with couples that when one spouse—in particular,

---

93 Since their other responsibilities may interfere with the timely performance of these *mitzvos*, women are not held to set times as men are; however, the Alter Rebbe did say that women are obligated to pray twice daily. The Alter Rebbe also held that women are obligated to know what is permissible by Jewish law and what is forbidden (which implies that they are obligated to learn Torah, in order to know this).

the wife—expresses patience, perseverance, and a deep commitment to the marriage, amazing turnarounds can often be achieved.

The Lubavitcher Rebbe teaches[94]:

There is a special mission given to women, each of whom is called (Psalms 113:9) akeres habayis, the "mainstay of the home," for the conduct of the entire home depends on her. Every Jewish home must be similar to the Sanctuary and Holy Temple in which G-d's presence resided. It must be pure and holy, so that G-d can say, "I dwell within them." Since the women are the "mainstay of the home," it is she [sic] who makes the home a sanctuary, similar to the Holy Temple of which G-d says, "I will dwell within them."

When a woman works to refine herself, she restores and preserves the purity within her family and helps create a home that is harmonious and beautiful. The reassuring presence of such a wife, whose faith in Hashem is firmly rooted, gives a man the ability to focus on his most important mission in life: to serve G-d and fulfill His will.

The Beginning of Wisdom

We recite in our morning prayers each day, *"Reishis chochmah yiras Hashem, sechel tov l'chol oseihem, tehilaso omedes law'ad,"* which translated literally means that "the

---

94 *Gutnick Chumash Vayikra*, based on a *sichah* of the Rebbe 27 of *Elul* 5742.

beginning of wisdom is the fear of G-d, good understanding is given to all their practitioners; His praise endures forever." But another possible interpretation is that when this verse is "*reishis*" or foremost in a woman's mind, her accumulating Torah wisdom (*chochmah*) will lead her to a greater awareness of G-d and a greater sense of awe (*yiras Hashem*) in His presence.

Every Friday night before Kiddush, we recite King Solomon's poetic homage to the "woman of valor" (Proverbs 31):

Her value far exceeds that of gems.

The heart of her husband trusts in her; he lacks no gain.

She treats him with goodness, never with evil, all of the days of her life.

She seeks out wool and flax, and works willingly with her hands.

She is like the merchant ships; she brings her food from afar.

She rises while it is still night, and gives food to her household and sets out the tasks for her maids.

According to one commentary,[95] this means that the woman of valor will, even at a time of "night", when the family is undergoing difficulties, transcend those difficulties

---

95   *Sefer Bechorei Aviv* citing *Hayehudi*.

with love and devotion, and provide the best that she can for her family.

Beauty Is In Your Eyes

Indeed, every woman has unique talents for rearing a family. She needs to appreciate the work she does for her family, and realize that her family appreciates her as well. Mrs. Chassida Mortner told the following story, which illuminates this point, at a mother-and-daughter tea at my daughter's school, *Bnos Menachem*.

A small boy once became lost in the woods. He began to cry loudly. The king happened to be passing by with his entourage, and he overheard the boy's cries. Halting his procession, he approached the child. "What's wrong?" the king asked.

"I'm looking for my mother," the boy replied. "I don't know where she is."

The king was moved by the boy's plight and said, "Come with me. Together we'll find her. Can you describe her?"

The boy sighed. "Her smile, her hair—everything about her is beautiful. She is the most beautiful woman in the whole world."

Back at the palace, the king sent out messengers to find a woman who fit the boy's description, but to no avail. No one had seen her. Then the king had an idea. He would have all the women of the kingdom come to the palace and walk past the boy, and he would surely recognize her.

The next day the palace was filled with housewives, shepherdesses and aristocrats. They lined up and one by one they strolled past the boy. As each one walked by, the boy sadly shook his head. Not one of them was his mother.

Suddenly in walked a pockmarked crone dressed in rags. Disgusted, the courtiers tried to throw her out, but the king insisted, "Let her have her turn."

When the woman hobbled by, the boy cried out, "Mommy!"

"My son!" the woman exclaimed. "I thought you were lost forever!" And they ran into each other's arms.

Although a woman may not be a flawless mother, her child still sees her as being perfect. Applying this idea to our own lives, whenever we feel that we may have fallen short of our standards, we should not allow the evil inclination to persuade us to despair. Instead, focus on the fact that even at such moments, your family still loves you. Consequently, when we see the imperfections of others (particularly in our own family), we should focus on continuing to love them wholeheartedly.

Exercises and Meditations

Visualize your soul accepting the assignment—willingly and happily—of coming down for the sake of elevating the soul of your husband, in order that you may be reunited again, eternally, in heaven. Consider the example of women such as Rachel, the wife of Rabbi Akiva, who so readily gave up honor and wealth, and whose devotion was so treasured by her husband. See yourself as being on that same level, in your devotion to your husband.

Points for Practical Reflection

- Women bear a major responsibility for creating a peaceful home.

- Women are the light in lives of their loved ones.

- The greater a woman's humility, the more she gains and the more she enables her loved ones to achieve their true potential.

- When a woman puts her husband's will first, he will strive to do her will.

- A wife with a strong faith in G-d gives her husband the ability to focus on serving Him.

- Realistic assessments and expectations of a relationship ensure that the relationship will endure.

8
—

Man's Role In Marriage

The Talmud (Shabbat 62a) states that "women are a separate people"—separate and different. Men will approach a problem with a different attitude and from a different perspective than women will, and vice versa. A husband and wife may disagree (at first) with what are considered essentials in a home, for example. Often what appears clear and simple to a husband will appear quite complex to his wife, and something that a woman understands almost automatically will be baffling to her husband.

Men and women are expected to utilize the particular strengths of their masculine and feminine nature to improve their marriages.

Humility and Men

Men should follow the example of our forefather Avraham, who said, "I am like dust" (Genesis 18:27). In the *Tanna D'bei Eliyahu*, Eliyahu (Elijah the Prophet) teaches that "man must be humble in his Torah learning, in good deeds, and in his fear of Heaven" in all his relationships—as a son, a husband, father, student, and neighbor—"in order that he should be beloved above and pleasant below and accepted by all." He explains that "when a man is humble...then his wife will fear him, and so to the members of his household, his neighbors and relatives, and also the non-Jews."[96]

This "fear" of him that will come upon others is more properly defined as "awe and respect", because "the Shechinah rests upon whoever is humble."[97] Whoever is in regular contact with a truly humble man can perceive that he is on a higher spiritual plane than others.

Masculine Strength

It is important not to confuse humility with timidity or weakness. It is neither. It is an acceptance of our particular strengths and abilities, along with an understanding of what is expected of us. It takes a great level of humility to admit that G-d knows better than we do what is good for us,

---

96   Chapter 15, quoted in "Who's the Man in the House?"

97   Ibid.

that G-d will give us what we need, and that we need what He has already given us—including the challenges in our marriage.

Men naturally tend to self-restraint. A man should therefore discipline himself to restrain his anger and to make a clear demonstration of his love for his wife. His appreciation for her will be strengthened if he reminds himself that his soul mate made the decision to descend once again into this world for his sake alone. (As mentioned in the preceding chapter, the *Zohar* teaches that although a man may have to be reincarnated to rectify his sins, women generally do not, for they accomplish their rectification in the higher worlds. However, the feminine soul often cannot bear to be separated from her mate and so she chooses to return to this world to serve as his helpmate, thus demonstrating an extraordinary degree of love and devotion.)

Obligatory Respect

Sometimes a husband is cold to his wife, or demands submission from her, and he assumes the attitude that he is the king of the house, whom the Torah says the wife must humbly obey. This is a grave error. He may be the king, but he has no right to be a tyrant. On the contrary, the Talmud (*Gittin* 6b) states that "A man should not project excessive fear in his household." The Rambam brings down (*Yad Hachazaka, Ishut*) that "a man shall honor his wife more than his own self and shall love her as he loves himself, and shall constantly seek to benefit her according to his means; that he shall not unduly impose his authority on her and shall speak gently with her; that he shall be neither sad nor irritable."

The Talmud stresses (*Yevamos* 62b) that a man "should always be careful to respect his wife more than himself."

Sima Basry clarifies[98]:

"Always" means under all conditions and circumstances.

What is the limit to this respect? Our Rabbis tell us: "the one who loves his wife as himself, who honors her more than himself and steers his children on the right path, is described in the verse (Job 5:24): 'And know that peace is in your tent.' Rabbi Chelbo said (Bava Metzia 59a) that a man should be careful to respect his wife, since only because of her is a blessing found in the home."

If no blessing is found in their home, her husband must strive to awaken her inner, feminine powers, through exalting and praising her. Therefore, Raba advised the citizens of Mehouza: "Honor your wives [that you may be enriched]!"

This actual connection between blessings in the home and the wife testifies to her great importance. This honor is very fundamental for the well-being of the family, since it sets the wife at a high level of status in the family.

98   Basry, pp.57-59.

A woman is very willing to do even the most difficult housework, however, she wants to feel like a queen in her own house; she wants to know that she holds an honored place in the eyes of her children and husband.

This will only happen when her husband realizes her goodness and is careful to tell her how he feels. There is no limit to the amount of thanks that a man is obligated to give his wife! "It would be enough were they [simply] to raise our children and save us from sin." (Yevamos 63b)

However, if a man does not honor her deeds [and] takes her work for granted and even becomes angry when something doesn't go the way he'd like, [then] her self-image will be lowered and she'll feel like a hired maid in her own home.

Therefore, our sages stressed that a man should honor his wife more than himself, because if his respect for her decreases, then so will his love for her.

Proper Honor

Honor can take many forms. One should follow the customs of the community, but consider your wife's specific tastes and try to cater to them, to the best of your ability and budget. Even more than gifts (not to minimize their importance!), a woman appreciates attention and affection.

A man has an obligation to demonstrate a tender regard for his wife. Toward this end, he should compliment his wife for both her physical and spiritual qualities. He is commanded by the Torah (Exodus 21:10) to provide her with "her food, her clothing, and her conjugal rights." Rabbi Yitzchak Ginsburgh clarifies that if a man does not compliment his wife in regard to these qualities, "it is questionable if he has truly satisfied her need for them. Part of his duty, then, is to praise her (in a sensitive and appreciative manner) for her prowess as a housekeeper (chiefly represented by her cooking), her taste in dress, and her physical attractiveness...."[99]

At our Shabbos table, my husband often tells newly-married men that he personally heard Rabbi Deitch (dean of the *Tzemach Tzedek Kolel Chabad* in Jerusalem) instruct a young husband to praise his wife no matter what. For instance, when she serves him fish, he should say, "I never tasted such delicious fish in all my life!" (Just be sure to actually taste the food first! A wife may find it hard to accept her husband's enthusiastic praise over the delicious taste of her food, if he has yet to take a single bite.)

A husband might think that complimenting his wife for her housekeeping, her cooking, or the way she dresses is petty. But such praise is crucial to a woman's sense of self, unlocking the reservoirs of her strength and helping her feel loved, appreciated, and joyful.

99   Ginsburgh, pp 148-149 (footnotes 34 and 35).

Wifely Support

A wife can be a man's greatest asset in life. With a wife's emotional support, a man can achieve well beyond what might rationally be expected of him. Very often, though, a woman is called upon to support the family financially as well as emotionally. In our times it is commonplace that many women work outside the home. Many women actually welcome a change from the home routine and the opportunity for interaction with other adults, in addition to the satisfaction they may derive from helping to pay the bills.

One's wife should not, however, be relied upon as the major breadwinner. Often, the financial advantage of a second income is minimized by the arrangements that may be necessary for the wife to work outside of the home: babysitting, housekeeping, conveniences. But more significantly, there are emotional drawbacks to relying on the wife to support the family: if she is earning more than the husband, it is quite possible that she will become the dominant partner in the relationship.

A man who is learning Torah while his wife works may be able to maintain his self-respect and the respect of others if his learning is going well. If, however, his wife is providing the bulk of their support, then it is likely that his self-esteem and the esteem in which his wife holds him, will suffer.

Kind Words Kindly Spoken

A husband should never speak unpleasantly to his wife. The Talmud states (*Bava Metzia* 59a) that "a man should always be on guard against causing his wife pain, since she is quick to cry." If a man does cause his wife pain and tears, he has transgressed the Torah prohibition (Leviticus 25:17) of "a man should not oppress his fellow."

Even if a man is not entirely happy with his situation, he ought to maintain a cheerful attitude. His wife will be comforted by his faith, and that will spread throughout the entire household. He should share his thoughts with his wife, so that she sees that her opinion is valued; yet he should be careful not to talk so much that his wife feels burdened by the conversations.

Some husbands barely find the time to converse with their wives. They may use as an excuse the injunction in *Pirkei Avos* (1:5), "Do not converse excessively with women, even your own wife." Yet the great Rabbi Akiva Eiger wrote in a letter after his first wife had passed away that "many times we had discussions on the subject of serving G-d which lasted half the night." [100]

Every night when the Lubavitcher Rebbe came home, no matter what the time, he would spend time with his wife, Rebbetzin Chaya Mushka. And every day he made an effort to have tea with her. The Rebbe told Dr. Ira Weiss,

---

100 Letter 109, quoted in Rabbi Yosef Tropper, *The Aishes Chayil Song* (TPress:2014).

the cardiologist who treated both the Rebbe and his wife, Rebbetzin Chaya Mushka, that "the time I do devote to have tea with my wife every day is as important to me as the obligation to put on tefillin every day."[101]

Sometimes a man may feel that he just doesn't have that much to discuss with his wife. He may believe that she is unable fully to understand or appreciate his deep thoughts on a Torah topic, or that she will not be interested in his workday activities. He may also misconstrue as disinterest her inability to sit still and focus on him while the baby is crying, the dishes need washing, and homework is waiting to be done.

As much as a man wants reassurance that he is the center of his wife's universe and as such deserves her undivided attention, he needs to be mature enough to realize that at times his wife's other responsibilities temporarily override his needs. He should be aware, though, that his wife genuinely welcomes these discussions, that she takes pride in his Torah learning, and that she feels comforted and complimented by his desire to share with her the events of his day.

101 Rabbi Mendel Kalmenson, *Seeds of Wisdom: Based on Personal Encounters With the Rebbe* (New York: Jewish Educational Media, 2013), p. 82.

Bring Her to Your Side

Women also want to feel that they are of paramount importance to their husband. A husband's positive attention, approval, and appreciation are necessary to a woman's emotional security. A harsh tone of voice, teasing, or criticism—even occasional or minor—can lead a woman to feel unappreciated and unloved. Similarly, a woman who is not criticized or teased, but is not included in her husband's daily life, can end up feeling ignored or neglected.

If a wife truly seems to be distancing herself from her husband, perhaps because she feels ignored or disrespected, a husband must do his utmost to bring her back. In this, as in all areas of marital life, he ought to use kindness rather than anger or force, for those tactics will only drive her farther away. He should refrain from criticism and instead praise his wife, showing her even greater honor and respect than he has up until this point. Being kind, considerate, loving, and giving will draw her close and keep her close.

If a wife seems always to be preventing her husband from doing what he wants to do, the husband should invest some time in self-examination. He should remember that in addition to being a soulmate, a wife is a "helpmate," as it says (Genesis 2:18): "I will make him a helper to match him (literally: against him)", and Rashi explains: "If he merits she is a 'helper', if he does not merit, she is 'against him.'" In this matter, his wife is simply acting as an agent of G-d, attempting to convey a message. That message might be that he is not treating her properly, or that his spirituality is in danger of lapsing.[102]

Once he begins to correct himself, he will see that his wife's opposition will markedly decrease, to the point that she becomes his strongest supporter. And as the Talmud tells us (*Sotah* 17a), the *Shechinah* feels welcome in a home that is graced with friendship, joy, and love between a husband and wife.

Exercises and Meditations

Recognize that your wife sacrificed her place in heaven to come down here for your sake. Visualize her as assisting angel, whose mission is to help you perfect yourself and thereby enable you to reunite with your soulmate in heaven. Resolve to help her complete her mission. Treat her with the gratitude and appreciation appropriate for such a gracious and loving gesture.

Smile at your wife and greet her pleasantly every morning.

Try to give your wife at least one sincere compliment daily.

Make it a habit to spend a certain amount of time every day, or at least once a week, conversing privately

102 Cf Rabbi Shalom Arush, *The Garden of Peace,* translated by Lazer Brody (Diamond Press, 2008).

with your wife. If possible, take a walk together. Even a short walk around the block will intensify your feelings of companionship and help you to focus on your status as a couple.

Consider your wife's personality and temperament. Try to imagine what sort of gift or gesture she would appreciate. Visualize all the steps necessary to procure or produce this wonderful item. Picture yourself presenting it to her; picture her reaction.

Points for Practical Reflection

- A husband is obligated to demonstrate care and concern for his wife.

- Treat your wife like a queen and she will treat you like a king.

- Honor and respect your wife more than yourself.

- Compliment her by sharing your time, your thoughts, and your daily life with her.

- Do not overly rely on your wife for financial support.

- If your wife is preventing you from doing what you want to do, examine your own actions.

- Correcting yourself will lead to your wife becoming your greatest supporter.

9
—

Unity

When you make the achievement of unity in your home a priority of the highest order, you are empowered by G-d to succeed in this transformation.

As mentioned earlier, you and your spouse have different temperaments and different innate traits. Each one of you, with your own wisdom and abilities, has a unique way of serving Hashem. Nevertheless, the two of you truly form a single unit. Having different roles should not imply any disunity in your relationship.

You can use the exemplary fraternal relationship of Moshe Rabbeinu and his older brother, Aharon, as a lodestar to guide you in your quest to establish a unity of common goals and values in your home.

Holy Oil

The unity between Moshe and Aharon represents the unity between the King and the *Kohen Gadol*, the High Priest, who officiated at the most important Temple services. From the unity of King and Priest there was a flow of blessings for all of Israel. As the psalm states (133:1-3): "Behold, how good and how pleasant it is for brothers to dwell together. Like the good oil upon the head, descending upon the beard, the beard of Aharon, descending upon the hem of his garments. It is like the dew of Hermon, which descends upon the mountains of Zion."

Both the king and high priest are anointed with oil, which is a lubricant. This is an indication that the relationship between them should be free of friction. The Talmud relates that when Moshe poured oil on Aharon's head to anoint him, two drops dripped onto Aharon's beard, where they hung and glittered like two shining pearls. As Aharon spoke, his beard moved and these two drops miraculously ascended until they reached the roots of his beard.[103]

Initially, when these two drops fell from Aharon's head to his beard, Moshe feared that he himself had defiled the

103 *Horayos* 12a.

sanctity of the oil by using too much. To allay Moshe's fears, a heavenly voice proclaimed: "It is like the dew of Hermon." Just as the dew on Mount Hermon is fresh and undefiled, so too the oil on Aharon's beard was not defiled.

As for Aharon, he worried that perhaps he had profaned the droplets on his beard. But a heavenly voice reassured him by proclaiming, "Behold, how good and how pleasant it is for brothers to dwell together." Just as Moshe was blameless, so was Aharon blameless. The message to the brothers was that their unity was so great that when the *Shechinah* spoke to one of them, it was an answer for both of them.

Our rabbis interpret this teaching in a spiritual sense[104]: Oil represents wisdom. Moshe had ascended Mount Sinai and lived there like an angel among angels for forty days. He thought, "Perhaps I was not using my wisdom properly. Perhaps I should have interacted more with the people." The heavenly voice told him, "No, you did not act improperly. None of your wisdom went to waste."

Aharon had a different concern. "I descended to the lowest stratum of society, concerning myself with the guidance of man's material and spiritual needs. Perhaps I should have stayed in seclusion so that I could learn more."

The heavenly voice proclaimed, "No, you too used your wisdom properly."

104 *Tehillim* Artscroll Tanach Series, Vol. 2, pp. 1588-1590.

The drops of oil ascending to the roots of Aharon's beard demonstrated that when Aharon used his wisdom to bring peace among the common folk, this was an appropriate and holy use of his wisdom.

The verse teaches that this oil reached Aharon's garments. "Like the good oil upon the head, descending upon the beard, the beard of Aharon, descending upon the hem of his garments."

The word used here for "garments," *midosav*, literally means "measurements." This is an appropriate description of the High Priest's costume because Jewish law requires that the High Priest's garments fit him precisely.

Unique Wisdom for Unique Missions

Middah is also the word for a character trait. The oil falling "upon the hem of his garments" indicates that Aharon's wisdom did not remain in the intellectual realm but, being wisely used, penetrated his soul and positively affected his character traits.

Thus we learn that both Moshe and Aharon served G-d by using their wisdom in their own ways. By doing so, each implemented his own talents to fulfill his unique mission. Nevertheless, they were united.

The message is clear. Both great leaders served Hashem in their own unique way. So too must a husband and wife serve in their own unique way.

When the Jewish people are in such a state of unity, then the cherubs atop the Holy Ark turn to each other in a fraternal fashion (Exodus 25:20): "Their faces were turned each one toward his brother." These cherubs represent the two leaders of the Jewish people: the King and the High Priest. When the king *Moshiach* comes, he will live in harmony with the High Priest.[105]

The Holy Fire of Man and Woman

The Hebrew words for "man" (*ish*) and "woman" (*isha*) each contain the letters *alef* and *shin*, which together spell *aish*, or "fire." This indicates that each spouse has his or her own fire. When they are not worthy, this is a fire of lust, envy or anger—characteristics that enter a couple's life when the Divine Presence is absent.

The word *ish* contains the letter *yud*, and the word *isha* contains the letter *hey*. When these two letters are combined, they spell one of Hashem's names. This indicates that when the couple refines their characters, that flame becomes a holy fire of love, and G-d dwells in their midst.[106]

---

105 Ibid.

106 Ginsburgh, p. 109.

Thus, the Sages teach, "If [a couple] merit"—if they refine themselves—"the Divine Presence dwells between them. But if they do not merit, [the Divine Presence withdraws, and] the fire [of this-worldly passions] devours them."[107]

Rabbi Ginsburgh elaborates[108]:

*Our Sages teach us (Yoma 21b) that there are six levels of fire, the lowest being physical fire and the highest being the fire of the Shechinah. This highest fire is referred to as **aish ocheles aish, "the fire that consumes all other fires."** When husband and wife merit this holy fire (when "the Divine Presence dwells between them"), then all other fires are consumed therein.*

[T]his highest fire corresponds to the ray (or "line," kav) of God's infinite light that permeates the vacuum created by the initial contraction (tzimtzum[109]) and brings all worlds and souls into being, sustains them, and ultimately bestows Divine consciousness on them.

Just as the kav enters the vacuum, so does the Shechinah enter the home and heart of a husband and wife who, by denying their own egocentricity, create "room" for the Shechinah to enter and "create" a new life within them.

Men and women have their own ways of actualizing this holy fire. Rabbi Ginsburgh teaches that:

---

107 *Sotah* 17a.

108 P. 111, footnote 4.

109 "The contraction and 'removal' of God's infinite light in order to allow for creation of independent realities" Ginsburgh, Glossary, p. 443.

The husband's holy fire is his 'intellectual light' (ohr sichli, the initials of which spell aish, "fire"), which he introduces into the home as the wisdom of the Torah.

...The wife's holy fire is her "complete faith" in G-d (emunah shleimah, the initials of which also spell aish, "fire"), expressed chiefly through her heartfelt prayers and blessings, as well as through her general attitude toward life. Her firm, enduring faith strengthens her husband and family, providing them with a warm hearth and protective refuge from the storms and vagaries of life. Her flame of faith penetrates and ignites the faith of her husband and family.

Husband and wife ideally inspire each other to contribute their respective qualities, each fanning the flames of the other's holy fire.[110]

The final letter of the phrase ohr sichli (associated with the man) is yud, whereas the final letter of the phrase emunah shleimah (associated with the woman) ends with the letter hei. When husband and wife realize their inner holy selves, these two letters combine to spell Hashem's name.

This indicates that when the Divine Presence dwells between them, it melts away the other "unholy fires" and makes it easier for the couple to continue to live a holy life. However, one should not be discouraged or dismayed if your spouse is not striving for holiness at the same rate that you are, or even attempts to impede your development. Work on fanning your own fire, and eventually your spouse will be

110 Ginsburgh, pp. 111-114.

warmed by it. The more effort you put into becoming holy, the more G-d will do for you.

Squeeze the Best Out of Yourself

The Alter Rebbe suffered tremendously before he was able to reveal his teachings of *Chassidus*. The Rebbe compared the imprisonment and the crushing struggles he endured to the process of the olive press: "Just as an olive gives forth its oil when it is squeezed and pounded, similarly, it was only through the accusations that took place in Petersburg that the essence was revealed."[111]

The same dynamic applies to our souls. As challenges come our way and we work through them, the more positive aspects of our soul get "squeezed out" and rise to the surface.

The following story illustrates how a trying situation can refine and transform a person's character:

During World War I, many Jews in Poland fled their hometowns. Rabbi Meir Chodosh—later to become the great mashgiach of Chevron Yeshiva—was one of these refugees. He and a friend walked to the outskirts of a neighboring village together, only to learn that the German army was advancing and that the terrified residents had begun loading their wagons in preparation for a hasty departure.

111 Rabbi Menachem M. Schneerson, *On the Essence of Chassidus* (New York:Kehot Publication Society, 1998) chapter 5, page 46.

The two men were about to board a wagon with some of the villagers, when Reb Meir's friend remembered that he had left his father's tefillin behind, and begged Reb Meir to wait for him while he retrieved them. Reb Meir agreed, and his friend hurried back to search for his father's tefillin.

A procession of wagons carrying the villagers and their possessions passed by as Reb Meir waited for his friend to return. As each wagon went past, its driver offered Reb Meir a ride, but Reb Meir declined, explaining that he was waiting for his friend. After some time, Reb Meir realized that soon no wagons would be left. Nevertheless, he continued to wait.

At last, his friend returned, just as the last wagon began to pull out. It had only one empty seat left. The friend jumped into the wagon along with his possessions, leaving Reb Meir behind alone.

Shocked, Reb Meir thought to himself, "I can't believe that after I waited so long, he didn't even try to share his seat with me." For a moment, he regretted having waited, but he then said to himself, "I'm not sorry I waited, because I know that I did the right thing."

In later years, he would tell his students, "At the moment that this pure thought entered my heart, I sensed that something had changed within me. From that day on, I became a better person."

The complex mix of emotions evoked in us by and towards our spouses is easily manipulated by our *yetzer hara*, which tries to prevent us from behaving as kindly to our close ones as we are able to. This idea is illustrated in the following story:

The Baal Shem Tov once took his disciples on a trip. They eagerly anticipated all sorts of spiritual delights, such as encounters with lamed vovniks *(thirty-six secret holy men) and other mystics. But to their dismay, when their wagon came to their destination, all they saw was a nondescript village populated with simple villagers. After some time passed, the Baal Shem Tov summoned his followers back into the wagon to return home.*

One of them asked, "Why did we travel so far to see these simple villagers?"

The Baal Shem Tov replied, "All of these people have attained the high spiritual level called 'mah'[112] *because of their great self-sacrifice."*

He explained to his students that some years before, a poor wayfarer passing through the village had been apprehended and imprisoned because of a debt that he was unable to pay. In those times, imprisonment was often a prelude to a death sentence. The villagers could not stand by and watch this man suffer such a fate, even though he was a stranger to them. So each one sold some of his essential belongings in order to raise enough money to pay the man's debt and redeem him from prison.

The Baal Shem Tov explained that this degree of self-sacrifice brings out the innermost level of a person's hidden soul.

---

112 See *Maamorim* 5679 pg. 557 and on.

When the students of the Baal Shem Tov understood this, they too praised the villagers for their extraordinary dedication.[113]

A selfless act you perform for another person—particularly if that person is your spouse—benefits yourself as well, because such an act elevates your soul to a much higher level.

The Closer You Are, the Harder It Is

Although one might think it is a greater display of selflessness to act as nobly as these villagers did for a complete stranger, in reality, it can be much more difficult to show such self-sacrifice and dedication for someone with whom we are intimately connected.

That may be why the Torah enjoins us (Deut. 15:7) to give charity to "your brother within your gates, within your land" before others: we must not neglect those closest to home—our family, our community, our country—in our desire to reach out to those in need.

113 See Dovid Sears, *The Path of the Baal Shem Tov* (Maryland: Rowman and Littlefield, 1997), p. 6.

Bring Vitality to Your Everyday Life

For more than fifteen years, my family and I lived in *Eretz Yisrael*. The first time that we as a family left, our intention was to be gone only for one or two months. Consequently, although I notified my close friends, I did not think it necessary to call many of my acquaintances—whom I ordinarily might not see for such a length of time—to say goodbye. Those I did see before we left, I took leave of rather casually.

My husband and I had traveled from Israel to Great Neck, New York with our newborn son to raise funds for the Chabad soup kitchen in the city of Ma'ale Adumim. We were also going to visit my sister, who was in her ninth month of pregnancy with her first child. On the day that she gave birth, she received the devastating news that her husband, who until then had seemed to be in excellent health, had been diagnosed with leukemia (from which he ultimately passed away).

The doctors assured us that with appropriate treatment my brother-in-law had an excellent prognosis. Nevertheless, I felt that my sister would need our emotional support and practical assistance, and so we decided to delay our return home to Israel for three months. These three months extended to six months.

After a year had passed and we had still not returned, I began to regret the unceremonious way in which I had left. Our stay ultimately stretched out to a year and a half.

Needless to say, this was a very challenging time for us, during which I missed my extended family and friends tremendously. When we finally returned to Israel and I was reunited with them, I felt especially loving toward them. Because we had been separated by such a great distance for so long, I felt the need to make the most of every such moment and hold on to these beautiful feelings of love.

As the days passed, I wished that I could "package" the unusually intense emotions that had surfaced during these reunions and recall them at will. I resolved to infuse the moments I share with my family members, close friends, and even casual acquaintances with greater intensity as a way of demonstrating how much I love and appreciate them. Bringing more passion and vitality into my day-to-day relationships became my new goal.

Splitting the Waters

Familiarity, even if it does not breed contempt, can certainly dampen the passion and dilute the vitality of our closest relationships. We may need to be reminded of the true beauty of our soul mate, in order to reinvigorate our feelings. The tale of the splitting waters can help.

Our sages teach that during the Six Days of Creation, G-d addressed the water and showed it the Jewish nation. He made the water promise that when it would see the Jewish nation at the time of the Exodus from Egypt, it would split for them and allow them to cross through it. Yet when that time came and the Jews stood before the Red Sea (the Sea of Reeds), the water did not split until it saw that they had brought with them the casket containing the bones of Yosef.[114]

Why did the water not immediately keep its word? The Lubavitcher Rebbe explains[115] that at the time the water made its promise, it saw the souls of the Jewish nation as they were then, pure and radiant. By the time of the Exodus, after so many years of enslavement, the majority of the Israelites had fallen to the spiritual depths and the water no longer recognized them.

See the Essence

Yet Yosef had remained faithful to G-d all the days of his life. The Hebrew word for "bone," *etzem*, can also mean "essence." He had retained his essential, pure self. Moshe now told the sea: "Just as you know that hidden within this casket lies Yosef's skeleton, representing his pure Jewish essence, so too must you know that standing here is the pure essence of the Jewish people, hidden within a superficial

---

114 *Midrash Yalkut Shimoni, Tehillim*, reprint ed., (Jerusalem: 1960), chap. 114.

115 Rabbi Menachem Mendel Schneerson, *Bosi Legani* (New York: Kehot Publication Society, 1977) chap. 3.

coarseness."[116] The water acknowledged the truth of Moshe's words and split on their behalf.

When you look at your spouse, you must try to see the ideal essence of his or her soul. The *Zohar* teaches that prior to entering this world, this essence was easily seen by husband and wife, and their love was so deep that they were not willing to depart from one another. [117] Even after they enter this world separately, they seek each other out until they miraculously find each other again, and marry.

Initially, spouses will experience a sense of joy and excitement at being reunited with their soul mate. In this world, however, they cannot see each other's essence as they did in heaven. Thus, as time passes, it is possible that a lack of appreciation for the miracle of having found each other may develop.

The Miracle of Your Marriage

Both Jewish and secular popular literature abound with inspirational stories of miraculous *shidduchim*, or of miraculous reunifications of couples who had been torn apart by war, natural disaster, or even a simple misunderstanding. Readers of such stories marvel at the Divine Providence that brought these couples together,

---

116 This detail was told to me by Rabbi Chaim Steinmetz, the *shaliach* of Sarasota, Fla.

117 *Lech Lecha* 85b.

and they often assume that the unusual circumstances of their history guaranteed that the couples in the stories lived "happily ever after" with nary a cloud on the horizon of their love.

Perhaps some of them did. But although most people recognize the miracles involved in these stories, they fail to realize that *every shidduch*—even their own, as uncomplicated and ordinary as it might seem to them—involves such miracles. It is just that not every miracle is obvious. We don't marvel at every sunrise and sunset, although each one is equally miraculous.

Make an effort not to take your own marriage for granted. Recognize the miracle that G-d has wrought for you. The thought of it should fill you with awe and wonderment. The realization that you have been reunited with your soulmate should help to reawaken your love and appreciation for your spouse.

Heavenly Gifts

One of the blessings recited at a wedding refers to "[G-d,] Who created joy (*sasson*) and happiness (*simcha*), bridegroom and bride, gladness, jubilation, cheer and delight, love and friendship, harmony and fellowship." The Lubavitcher Rebbe teaches[118] that the first two joyful attributes are a gift from G-d to the couple, and thus

118 *Maamor Asher Boro* 5739.

appear as a unit before the phrase, "bridegroom and bride." In Hebrew, *sasson*, "joy" and *simcha*, "happiness" refer respectively to the external and internal manifestations of happy feelings. G-d therefore is blessing the couple with the potential for complete happiness with each other. The remaining eight attributes must be earned by the couple.[119]

Thus, a happy marriage is a result of effort in the face of personal challenge, which refines a couple and brings to therefore the resources contained in the depths of their souls.

Exercises and Meditations

Consider two disparate elements which, although very different from each other, unite to form a new and beautiful substance, for example honey and lemon into lemonade.

Visualize the love flowing between the brothers Moshe and Aharon and unifying them, although they were different men with different ways of serving Hashem. Now visualize the love flowing between you and your spouse and unifying the two of you, although you are different human beings with different ways of seeing the world and of serving Hashem.

---

119 Of these eight attributes, the first four refer to the physical pleasures a couple may enjoy when permissible, while the last four refer to the pleasures attainable by a couple without physical closeness. See *One Plus One Equals One*, by Rabbi Emanuel Feldman (Jerusalem: Feldheim, 1999).

Think of the ways in which your spouse differs from you, and how that complements you and completes your home. Consider these differences as blessings.

Visualize yourself at home in a very relaxed state. You are aware of the different elements within each individual in your home and you are at peace with them. In this state of serenity, you are able to focus on the virtues of peace in the home. An aura of humility surrounds you, and a yearning for unity within your family that spreads throughout your home. The holiness of your humble thoughts, speech and actions invite G-d's presence. You feel the warmth of holiness brilliantly radiating throughout your home. There is goodness within all elements of your home. You are happy.

Visualize a holy fire within yourself and a holy fire within your spouse. See each of these fires as taking on the shape of a Hebrew letter (*yod* for the husband and *hei* for the wife). Now they join together to form a name of Hashem. Experience yourself and your spouse as two parts of a whole, blended together. Feel that Hashem is dwelling in your midst.

Visualize yourself in a pressurizing, challenging situation. Imagine that as the pressure increases, it is refining and drawing forth your finest qualities, which may have been hidden until now even from your own knowledge. Know that these strengths are now available for you to utilize at any time.

Visualize yourself accepting a large gift-wrapped box. See yourself opening it up with delighted anticipation.

Inside you find two beautiful bottles, one marked "joy" and the other "happiness." Imagine that these two bottles are always full and always available for you to pour out some of these feelings and incorporate them into your daily life.

Write down the story of your meeting, courtship, and marriage. Read it as though it were fiction concerning people you don't know. Make note of how G-d directed events for the "characters." Recognize the miracles of your relationship.

Points For Practical Reflection

- Serve Hashem in your own unique way.

- Encourage your spouse to do so as well.

- Be aware that the efforts of the two of you complement each other.

- Make the achievement of unity in your home a top priority.

- Refining your characters brings a holy fire of love into your lives, and allows G-d to dwell in your midst.

- Challenges can "squeeze out" fine qualities of character within our souls.

- Every couple begins married life with a gift of joy and happiness from G-d.

- With the right attitude and the proper effort, a couple can adorn themselves with more joyous attributes throughout their lives together.

- When husband and wife act unselfishly toward each other, they merit that the *Shechinah, aish ocheles aish*, "the fire that consumes all other fires," dwells between them.

10

Why Can't We Get Along?

If you and your spouse really are not getting along, does that mean you were not meant to be together? No. Sometimes two people who are genuine soul mates are actually incompatible. It may be that a soul was destined to endure a difficult marriage as a means of rectification, either of one spouse or of their offspring. [120] As the saying goes, "A smooth sea never made a skillful sailor."

The difficulties in some marriages may arise from deep and invisible roots. We (generally) are not privy to the details of our hidden distant past, but knowing that it may be the possible cause of our present problems can ease

120 See *Yevamos* 63b.

our situation and cast it in a more positive light, as in the following story[121]:

There was once a chassid of the Alter Rebbe who was married to a miserable, wretched woman. Never once did a kind word pass her lips, only curses and imprecations. It particularly irked her whenever her husband traveled to the Rebbe; she would follow him down the road, shouting insults and berating him as he made his way.

After many years of abuse the poor man had had enough. He went to the Alter Rebbe and poured out his heart. The Rebbe listened to the man's tale of woe, his holy head resting on his arms.

"Take heart, my son," the Alter Rebbe said, raising his head. "Know that you are a reincarnation of a soul that lived in the times of our Judges and worshipped idols, as it states, 'And the people of Israel did evil in the sight of G-d, and served the idol of baal.' Our Sages explain (in Tractate Beitzah 25b) that the Jews worshipped idols seven times a day, and that each act of idol worship is punishable by death. When your case came before the Heavenly Court it was decided that you should marry this evil woman, a punishment worse than death. Thus you should be happy, not sad! For each time you are cursed and insulted, it is considered Above as if you had received the death penalty."

The chassid left much consoled.

---

121 Rabbi Rafael Nachman Kahn, *Extraordinary Chassidic Tales* (New York: Otsar Sifrei Lubavitch, 1997) vol. 3, pp 48-49.

Common Causes of Discord

Most marital difficulties are of more readily discernible origins. Some extremely common issues are: differing levels of religious observance, maintaining double standards, problems dealing with money, and different expectations and styles of parenting.

Religious Differences

While it may be distinctly uncomfortable for spouses to be on differing levels of religiosity, it is not an insurmountable obstacle to a good relationship. Spirituality is not an unchangeable constant, and the maintenance and development of our spiritual side takes effort. One spouse may not see the need to put in that effort as strongly as the other does, but that view is always subject to change.

If you wish to go further in your religious observance but meet with resistance from your spouse, do not make it into an issue between you. Our Sages have taught us that before every soul descends to this world it is made to swear an oath (*Niddah* 30b): "Be righteous, and do not be wicked", and the *Chassidic* masters explain this to mean "Don't be wicked with your righteousness."[122] Don't use

---

122 See Rabbi Shalom Arush, *The Garden of Peace: A Marital Guide for Men Only* (Diamond Press: 2008).

your newfound righteousness as a basis for arguments, criticism, and marital discord.

Concentrate on your own development, and accept your spouse as he or she is. In such cases the gentle influence of example is often stronger than the resistance. (If your spouse is actively interfering with your compliance with *halachah*, consult with your rabbi as to the proper way to proceed. Your rabbi may suggest that you take leniencies in areas in which you wish to be more stringent. The Rebbe in many instances told one partner to hold off on accepting upon themselves certain rituals for which their spouse was not ready.)

Double Standards

As mentioned earlier, people often apply double standards without realizing that they are doing so; if they do realize it, they rationalize the imbalance. For example, a woman may take offense when her husband spends time away from her, but sees nothing wrong in spending an equal amount of time with her friends. Or a husband may criticize his wife for being a spendthrift because she has purchased a new outfit, yet consider his $100 bottle of fine wine to be an essential expenditure.

If pressed, each will defend their actions as necessary or harmless. However, a person who applies double standards is devaluing his or her spouse, who may become disgusted with the apparent injustice. They then may feel justified in redressing the imbalance through a deliberate similar action of their own. And a vicious cycle has begun.

Monetary Dealings

Double standards are often apparent in financial matters, as in the example above. Problems related to dealing with money may manifest in behaviors such as greed (an inability to control spending) or as stinginess (an inability to spend even when necessary).

In regard to greed, we learn that before an animal is brought as an offering, its fat must be removed. Certain fats are permissible to eat, others are forbidden; certain pleasures are holy and permissible, others are prohibited. In his *Likkutei Sichot,* [123] the Alter Rebbe explains that fat is symbolic of physical pleasures. If someone errs unintentionally by eating forbidden fat, it indicates a (perhaps subconscious) tendency toward a prohibited pleasure. A person has to uproot the greedy desire for such pleasures. Otherwise, personal selfishness can destroy the marital bond. For instance, a woman who is in endless pursuit of material things is likely to continually compare her situation unfavorably with that of others. She may then accuse her spouse of being a poor provider, and he in turn is likely to feel devalued or inadequate.

123 Vol. 3, pp. 944-946.

A second money-related problem is excessive worry. Sometimes a spouse—more often than not, the husband—is financially successful but fearful that spending even one penny more than necessary will exhaust his savings, depriving him of adequate resources for unexpected bills and a comfortable retirement. Typically, such a husband micromanages his wife's spending on household expenses and berates her even when she buys necessities. He may force her to go to work when that is not necessary and then take every penny that she earns, giving her the bare minimum as an allowance.

People who have an unhealthy relationship with money—whether they are stingy or spendthrifts—need to work on this issue if they are sincere about promoting peace in their home. Professional counseling may prove useful in helping those so afflicted to achieve healthier and more functional perspectives.

If neither you nor your spouse spend or save excessively, but you are nonetheless experiencing financial woes because despite your efforts, your income simply is not adequate to cover your family's basic, reasonable needs, you must be careful not to allow this to harm your relationship. Attempt to deal with the situation in a calm manner, pursuing all reasonable avenues of assistance, and not descend into blaming or shaming one another. It is essential to remember that you are partners, and that such a situation is one of the challenges designed by G-d specifically to strengthen your partnership.

Put a Good Slant on Your Marriage

In his book *VeDibarta Bam*, Rabbi Moshe Bogomilsky offers the following insight[124]:

> When a couple set out to make a home, the Torah requires a mezuzah to be placed on the entrance. On the outside of the mezuzah is [the Hebrew letter] "shin," which represents Hashem's name of Sha-dai.... According to the Kabbalists, this name is also an acrostic for the words Shomer Daltot Yisrael, "The protector of Jewish homes."
>
> In addition to the spiritual powers of the mezuzah which bring protection and success to the home, the mezuzah constantly implies a very important lesson to the residents and those who enter into the home.
>
> When a mezuzah is affixed to the doorpost, it is placed on a slant. The simple reason for this is that there is a difference of opinion in halachah whether the mezuzah should be affixed vertically or horizontally. To satisfy both opinions, a compromise is made by putting it on a slant (Yoreh Dei'ah 289:6).
>
> Perhaps it can also be said that there is a homiletic message conveyed by affixing the mezuzah on a slant.
>
> If one wants the home to be protected, if one wants the home to be long lasting, then everyone must bend a little bit.

To bend is to be understanding; to try to empathize with your spouse. If each spouse is unyielding and makes

124 *Rosh Hashanah*, pages 22-23.

no effort to understand the other partner's position, their home may have to endure real difficulties. However, if there is understanding and both partners are willing to bend and compromise, their home will be blessed with harmony and joy.

The popular expression, "to put a different slant on things," means "to gain a different perspective." Looking at a situation through the perspective of our spouse can change it for the better. During moments of challenge or crisis, however, this shift in perspective is not easy to maintain. Therefore, every day, at a time when you are not in turmoil or under stress, you should practice empathizing with your spouse.

Surpass Your Limits For Your Family

The Lubavitcher Rebbe often mentioned that in previous generations, the observance of such basic *mitzvos* as keeping kosher, observing the Sabbath, and providing a Jewish education for one's children required enormous personal sacrifices, sometimes to the point of risking one's livelihood or personal safety. In our times, when we are fortunately rarely put to such tests, we have an opportunity to demonstrate our commitment to Hashem through a different type of self-sacrifice. The Rebbe stated that just as Hitler, *yemach shemo* (may his name be blotted out), sought to destroy every Jewish soul, we can act with the same intense passion to seek out every Jewish soul and bring it back to Hashem. It's imperative that we dedicate ourselves wholeheartedly to the *mitzvah* of helping our fellow Jews [return to the path of Torah]. This sacrifice is just as pleasing to Hashem as that of the earlier generations, if not more so.

Rebbetzin Esther Jungreis, founder of the Hineni outreach organization, has published stories of the enormous dedication demonstrated by her parents on behalf of other Jews during the Holocaust. In her book *The Jewish Soul on Fire*, she asks the following rhetorical question: If during those turbulent times people were willing to risk their lives to save the life of a single Jew, why shouldn't we make similar sacrifices now to save the *soul* of a Jew? In doing so, we fulfill our Jewish character, epitomized by Hillel's famous motto (*Pirkei Avos* 1:14): "If I am only for myself, then what am I?"

When I read this, after connecting to Chabad, I thought, "If this is how we should act for strangers, how much more must we go the extra mile for our family members, and push ourselves to do whatever possible to help those closest to us get close again to Hashem and His ways."

Soul Levels

Often, when guiding a contentious couple, I discuss with them the concept of "soul levels." It is possible that a person has a "newer-level" soul, one that is comparable to a first-grader, as opposed to a soul that is comparable to a high school graduate or a college professor. Some souls are "newer" with much more work to accomplish. Just as you would not grow irate at a first grader who does not understand graduate level mathematics, so too you should not get angry at your spouse for his or her faults.

Other souls are in their last incarnation. They have refined themselves over the years and have only a small amount of improvement remaining to complete.

Become a Vessel for G-d's Light

The higher the level of a person's soul, the greater the amount of G-dly light one will receive. [125] Consequently, though, the challenge of achieving emotional stability and balance will also be greater, for such a person may have difficulty absorbing that light, as explained in the following passage from *Kuntres Uma'ayan*[126]:

> *Then the physical vessels, brain and heart, will be incapable of containing the overwhelming light of intellect and emotion, and the vessels will be harmed. Many people suffer incapacities, mental and emotional disorder, caused by an*

125 See earlier chapter. The Rebbe Rashab teaches in *Kuntres HaTefilah* that a person becomes a more worthy vessel by engaging in *hitbonenut* (deep contemplation) to internalize the G-dly light of his learning so that it will affect his animal soul. If that *hitbonenut* is missing, the inspiration that a person's G-dly soul experiences while in the midst of prayers or Torah learning has no influence on the animal soul.

126 Rebbe Rashab, *Kuntres Uma'ayan*, ch. 3:46.

overabundance of "light" and a paucity of "vessels," absorptive capacity.

As an example, picture in your mind a fine crystal champagne glass. The delicate goblet would be perfectly appropriate on a fancy dinner table, catching the jet of sparkling liquid as it spills forth from the bottle. Yet imagine this same vessel set at the foot of the raging waters of Niagara Falls: it would not only be useless there as a receptacle to catch and hold the cascading waters of the falls, but the glass itself would be shattered almost instantly by the overwhelming force of the torrent.

Thus, as we see here and as we discussed earlier, a person's apparent defects can be an indication of a high-level soul and a great potential for holiness. I tell my clients that they are presumably such people, and that they are experiencing problems in their relationship because they are not internalizing the light and energy that is flowing down to them.

In order to realize their higher-level soul potential and heal themselves and their relationship, I suggest that they take the steps necessary to build a great vessel needed to contain this "holy light." To do so, they need to add holiness to their lives by performing more *mitzvos*—particularly, profound study of the inner aspect of Torah (namely, *Chassidus*)—as well as meditation and prayer. Only then can real healing occur.

Nourish Your Soul

Even after you see improvement in yourself or your spouse, be careful not to return to the old habits of neglecting davening and Torah learning. Just as a person needs to eat every day and cannot dismiss hunger by saying that he ate a week ago, so too a person cannot say that he does not need to learn Torah now, since he did so last week. The soul needs daily nourishment to stay healthy and balanced.

I'll never forget a client whom I met on one of my trips back to Israel.

Because of major delays at the airport, I arrived at my home only minutes before candle lighting on the eve of *Rosh Hashanah*. On the second day of Rosh Hashanah, the children and I joined my husband on the street as he blew *shofar* for those who had been unable to attend synagogue. One of the people who came to hear him blow *shofar* was an acquaintance of mine whom I hadn't seen in more than three years. She told me that she had to see me that very night. As I hadn't really settled in yet, I replied that I would be happy to see her the next morning. But she insisted that it was critical to meet as soon as possible, so I relented.

When we met late that night, she told me that a friend of hers was in a state of crisis. "She began having panic attacks about a year ago. She's been seeing therapists and psychiatrists who have prescribed all kinds of medications, but nothing's helped." The woman was feeling acutely depressed. My friend begged me to see her that night and despite my jet lag, I agreed.

When I met this woman, I assumed that she wasn't religiously observant, as she was wearing slacks and her hair was uncovered, although she was married. I hesitated to speak freely because I was afraid that if she thought I was shoving religion down her throat or taking too mystical an approach to her very down-to-earth problem, she would dismiss my advice out of hand.

Suddenly, for some reason, I decided to be direct, and I began to tell her about the concept of bringing healing by making oneself a greater vessel for spirituality. I chose *mikveh* observance as the example by which to explain this concept. As soon as the words came out of my mouth, though, I regretted the choice, thinking it would have no relevance to her. But before I could stop and offer another example, she stared at me in shock and said, "I can't believe you said that."

Taken aback, I waited for her to explain. She was so emotional that it was hard for her to speak. "Tell me," I insisted gently.

She took a deep breath and began. "I used to go to the *mikveh* until about a year ago. Then I began to have irregular bleeding, and I had to go so often that I got fed up and stopped going altogether."

Amazed, I asked her when her panic attacks had begun.

She stood there, almost frozen, and said, "My goodness, just about the time I stopped going to the *mikveh*."

I blessed her that she should immediately make a decision to return to her previous commitment, and moreover go to a *mikveh* teacher in order to review the precise *halachic* requirements for preparing for immersion. Then and there she committed herself to doing so.

That night when she returned home, her panic attacks disappeared, along with her depression. She phoned me later to share the good news and said that her children—who had not seen her smile for almost a year—were delighted to have their mother back to herself.

The following week, at her request, I accompanied her back to her place of work and I saw with my own eyes her co-workers' amazement at her transformation.

Spiritual Factors

Had I not witnessed this story myself, I would not have believed it. But I did witness it—and many other similar miracles. When a disorder results from spiritual factors, those factors must be addressed. Although making yourself an adequate vessel for the light of holiness may seem tangential and even irrelevant to the problems you are facing, it may actually be the most powerful factor affecting the state of your marriage.

(Note: As mentioned in the Introduction, at times medication may be necessary to stabilize an emotional or psychiatric imbalance, especially if there is any danger to oneself or others. At other times medication is in order to help a person become focused and receptive to getting necessary treatment and information. In such cases, I do not hesitate to refer clients to the appropriate professionals. To do otherwise would be dangerously naïve as well as unethical.)

Exercises And Meditations

When you see a character flaw in yourself, say the following affirmations:

"This behavior just shows how holy I really am."

"G-d willing, I will soon channel these holy energies to the good."

When you see a character flaw in your spouse, say the following affirmations:

"This behavior just shows how holy my spouse really is."

"G-d willing, he/she will soon channel these holy energies to the good."

Try not to react to a difficult marital situation with self-pity; try not to focus on feeling disrespected, unloved, dissatisfied, or mistreated. Please do not castigate yourself for having made a bad choice of spouse. Instead, change your paradigm from "me" to "we."

Rewrite your internal script along the following lines: "*We* are here to help *each other* gain true respect, love, and honor. Working *together*, *we* can experience joy and happiness, and *our* relationship can be adorned with the other joyous attributes mentioned in the wedding blessing. If *we* haven't yet achieved these goals, *we* are unlikely to advance *our* cause by focusing on what's missing. With determination, hard work, and love, *we* will see positive results."

Actively work on increasing the spirituality in your life and home. A wife may try to ensure that the home is quiet enough for her husband to learn there or that it is sufficiently under control for him to go out to learn. A husband may make it possible for his wife to have more time to *daven* and learn Torah on her own by sharing responsibility for household chores or, if it can be afforded, by hiring someone to help with the housekeeping. (The Lubavitcher Rebbe was once asked if folding one's *tallis* (prayer shawl) right after Shabbos is a *segulah* (a good omen) for *shalom bayis*. The Rebbe replied that helping clean the dishes is a better *segulah*.) Or, a couple may learn Torah together.

Points For Practical Reflection

- An incompatible couple may still be genuine soul mates.

- Marital difficulties may be a rectification for a soul.

- Focus on your position as one of a couple, not an individual: "we" rather than "me."

- Increasing your spirituality can be an effective aid to your relationship.

- Not every soul is on the same level, and certain behaviors may be indicative of the soul's level.

- A "high level" soul requires more maintenance, or more nourishment, to complete its mission here.

11

Compassion And Forgiveness

In any relationship, it is imperative to look beyond the surface.

In the earlier days of the Chabad movement in America, there was a man who believed that the fervent devotion of certain chassidim to the Rebbe was inordinate and detracted from their relationship with G-d. He grew so incensed that he went to the Rebbe and demanded that he tell these chassidim to desist.

The Rebbe responded: "This is my fault. I love them so much that they love me in return."[127]

---

127 Weekly *Kfar Chabad* issue #1084 (inside back cover).

Not all of these chassidim were saintly. Yet the Rebbe had the ability to look into their souls and recognize their beautiful inner qualities.

You too can develop that ability, and recognize the beautiful inner qualities of your spouse.

Compassion Brings Love

Compassion banishes hatred and increases love. We learn this from a homiletic reading of the verse (Isaiah 29:22), "[Hashem says to] the house of Yaakov, he who redeemed Avraham."[128] The Alter Rebbe explains that Yaakov is associated with the trait of compassion and Avraham with the trait of love. Acting compassionately "redeems" and liberates the trait of love for G-d that may have become trapped deep within a person.

The person may be stuck at a particular point of spiritual and emotional development, unable to move forward. The Zohar teaches us that when you have compassion toward this person for being "stuck," those feelings of compassion are the tool that can "redeem" and help release the imprisoned soul. Once liberated, that soul

---

128 See *Tanya* Vol. 1, *Likkutei Amarim*, chap 32, page 429. Although the literal meaning of the verse is "Therefore, thus said the Lord Who redeemed Avraham, to the house of Yaakov . . . ," the *midrash* offers various alterative explanations, including the concept that Avraham was redeemed for the sake of Yaakov (that is to say, so that the Jewish nation would come into existence).

can then love Hashem more freely and act more lovingly toward His creations.

We are able to empower ourselves as well. When we have compassion on someone, a feeling of love toward them is aroused within us rather than a feeling of hatred. You may be finding it difficult to feel loving towards your spouse, due to his or her behavior or to some internal struggle of your own. Yet you can overcome this lack of love with compassion. As Rabbi Yaakov Y. Herman famously said, "If you have *rachmanus* (compassion), you don't need *savlanus* (tolerance)."[129]

Let the Past Pass

If the winds of disdain continue to blow through your marriage, ask yourself if you have done your utmost to fulfill the *mitzvah* of loving your fellow as yourself in regard to your spouse. One significant step toward the actual achievement of these high goals is to let go of the negative feelings and resentments one may harbor against one's spouse for past mistakes. You may feel tempted to maintain and nurture these feelings, but that is likely to increase the emotional distance between the two of you. Your spouse may feel rejected, which may well discourage him or her from attempting to change for the better.

---

129 Ruchoma Shain, *All for the Boss*, (New York: Feldheim, 1984) pg. 371.

We should rather, as *Tanya* teaches,[130] emulate the ways of Yosef (Joseph), who, when he was in a position to harm his brothers who had caused him great misery by selling him into slavery, instead displayed magnanimity towards them and treated them kindly.[131] This is one of the reasons for which the Talmud refers to him as "Yosef HaTzaddik, Joseph the righteous one."

Forgiveness is Kindness

The Lubavitcher Rebbe explains that just as Yosef forgave his brothers and repaid their treachery with kindness, so too can we repay with kindness even someone who has offended us. This is especially true regarding family members; if the offending party expresses sincere regret, one can welcome the opportunity to repair the relationship.[132]

When Shimi ben Geira cursed King David (II Sam. 16:10), King David did not respond angrily. Instead, he excused Shimi's actions, explaining, "For G-d told him, 'Curse!'" The Alter Rebbe uses this incident to prove that we must understand that "[w]hatever that person did to you

---

130 *Likkutei Amarim* Vol 1, chap 12, page 184.

131 Genesis 37-47; *Zohar*, Vol. 1, pg. 201a.

132 Judaism does not advocate that a person "turn the other cheek" when he is wronged. When a person is attacked or threatened by his enemies, he is enjoined to defend his rights, even if it means engaging in war. However, when a person has conflicts with members of his family or other Jews—who are considered members of his extended family—he should be magnanimous and always seek to resolve the conflict.

ultimately stems from G-d. The person was merely an agent from G-d, Who decreed that the thing should occur to you. Thus, since 'everything that G-d does is for the good,'[133] you must repay the person—who brought this 'good' to you—with kindness."[134]

If we are hurt by the words of another, we can try our best to remind ourselves that at that moment "a glimmer of the Divine Presence has vested itself within that person."[135] Work on not being angry with the messenger, because he was chosen by Hashem to relate His message to us. (The other person could choose not to accept such a mission, but that is not relevant to us, because we needed to hear the message anyway.)

Rather, if we can accept such incidents as coming from G-d, we can appreciate the opportunity they afford us to cleanse and elevate our soul, and to prove our loyalty and faith in G-d.

Acknowledge Your Past and Your Pain

One who refuses to relinquish past hurts in their marriage, forfeits the opportunity to repair and reinvigorate their most

133 *Brachos* 60b.

134 Miller, *Gutnick Edition Chumash*, paraphrasing a discourse from the Lubavitcher Rebbe that originally appeared in *Likkutei Sichos*, 28:138ff.

135 *Lessons in Tanya*, pp. 75-76.

important relationship. This is certainly not to imply that one should dismiss or deny the pain caused by these hurts. G-d forbid! We are human and we make mistakes, but we can deal with these mistakes in a productive and positive way.

The Torah provides us with the knowledge with which to counter the evil inclination. Our *yetzer hara* constantly tries to have us dig deeper into the abyss of despair or guilt. Move away from the irrational idea that our challenges are our fault or the fault of our spouse. Instead, exert the energy to internalize the knowledge of Torah and direct it toward benefiting from our challenges.

Each person has the right to their emotions during difficult times, and no one can say "Don't feel that way." But there comes a point at which continued grief, anger, resentment, guilt, or shame are unhealthy, and then it is time to unravel the heaviness of pain and move forward.

Never think that it is too late or will take too long. This realization came to me when I was nearing 40. Instead of feeling terrible that for so many years I lacked a the mystical teachings of Torah, I focused on being thankful that it had at last come my way. And I didn't have it until then for reasons only G-d knows.

Love is the acceptance of our imperfections. It's very easy to reject others for their imperfections and weaknesses, but that leads to a very lonely life. To love is to be kind, to give, and to forgive.

The Benefits of Forgiveness

Should you find yourself unable to change your perspective and feelings about your spouse, be patient with yourself. Continue to study the benefits of forgiveness, and you will be more likely to overcome your resistance toward forgiving your spouse.

The Lubavitcher Rebbe teaches[136]:

Even after the Jewish people criticized Moshe heavily, resulting in a punishment of venomous snakes, we nevertheless find that Moshe did not bear a grudge and prayed for the people to be saved. "From here we learn," writes Rashi, "that if a person asks you for forgiveness you should not be cruel and refrain from forgiving."

Rambam discusses the laws of forgiveness in three separate places in his *Mishneh Torah*: in *Laws of Personal Injury, Laws of Moral Conduct*, and *Laws of Teshuvah*. The Lubavitcher Rebbe explains that these describe three levels of forgiveness.[137]

In *Laws of Personal Injury*, Rambam teaches that "if one injures another, even if he paid full compensation … he does not achieve atonement for the sin that he committed until

136 Ibid.
137 Ibid.

he seeks out the injured party and is granted forgiveness from him."[138]

Rambam here describes the one who was hurt as "the injured party" and speaks of the "forgiving" of the injury. This is a type of forgiveness that absolves the perpetrator from being punished for a specific injurious act.

In terms of your marriage, this means that if your spouse has acted wrongly so that you are the "injured" party, when you forgive your spouse, he or she will be spared heavenly punishment.

Secondly, in *Laws of Moral Conduct*, Rambam states: "If the one [who sinned] returns and asks him for forgiveness, then he should forgive, for the forgiver should not be cruel."[139]

The focus here is not on the sin and its atonement, but rather on the character of the one who was offended. Here the victim is described as the "forgiver." He should not just forgive the particular sinful act, but the sinner, so that no trace of bad feeling remains.

In terms of your marriage, when you forgive your spouse in this way, you erase all traces of bad feelings that divide the two of you, and you improve your own character.

---

138 Rambam, *Mishneh Torah, Laws of Personal Injury* 5:9-10, as translated in the *Gutnick Edition Chumash, Numbers*, 4:167.

139 *Mishneh Torah* 6:6. Translation from Gutnick, *Numbers*, p. 167.

Thirdly, in *Laws of Teshuvah,* Rambam speaks of the highest level of forgiveness. He writes: "A person … should forgive … with a full heart and a willing spirit."[140]

At this level, the forgiveness is so deep that the sin is totally uprooted, as if had never occurred. Rambam thus here refers to the victim simply as "a person," no longer as an "injured party," since he has uprooted the damage as if it never happened. This law of forgiveness is found in the *Laws of Teshuvah*, repentance, to teach us that when a person forgives, it helps the perpetrator do *teshuvah*. Therefore, a person allows himself to be appeased because he knows that this will help the sinner come closer to Hashem and repent of his lapses.

Transformational Forgiveness

In terms of your marriage, when you forgive your spouse so profoundly that you do not even bear in mind his or her failings, you help your spouse transform him- or herself for the better.

In sum, when you forgive your spouse, 1) you prevent him or her from being punished from heaven, 2) you develop and refine your own moral character, and 3) you increase the likelihood that your spouse will do *teshuvah*. In addition, your own sins are forgiven, in keeping with our

---

140 *Mishneh Torah* 2:9-10, Translation from Gutnick *Numbers*, p. 167.

Sages' statement, "Whoever passes over his feelings, all his sins are passed over."[141]

It is clear, therefore, that when you deal with frictions in your marriage by forgiving your spouse, you attain immense rewards.

Forgiving Your Spouse

Forgiving your spouse is a vital aspect of maintaining peace in the home. As a first step to doing so, gain awareness of your own attitude by making it a habit to observe how willing or unwilling you are to forgive your spouse (especially if he or she has a hard time admitting guilt and offering an apology).

The foundation of forgiveness is empathy for and an understanding of the challenges that your spouse faces. Consider that the daily stresses and demands on a person's time and energy prevent him or her from engaging in the spiritual practices that sustain us, and that without that nourishment it becomes difficult to access and demonstrate one's kinder, more loving side. An increased involvement in worldly affairs often strengthens our negative tendencies.

In the *Refa'ainu* ("Heal us") blessing in the *Amidah*, we ask G-d to grant a speedy recovery not only to those who are suffering from a physical illness but also to those who

---

141 *Rosh Hashanah*, 17a.

are suffering from illnesses of the soul. In that prayer, you can add the names of anyone you find difficult to forgive. You can ask G-d to hasten the healing of that person's soul so that his or her traits become refined, as befits a creature created in the image of G-d.

At the same time, you should ask G-d help you develop the strength and patience to forgive and deal with that person in a healthy and dignified manner. Lastly, do not forget to get into the habit of apologizing sincerely when you are in the wrong, and to graciously accept your spouse's apology when offered (whether it sounds sincere or not).

G-dly Vitality

You might ask why you should feel compassionate or forgiving towards your spouse, if he or she is consistently annoying you or causing you pain?

Your spouse might not be receiving the G-dly vitality that he or she needs, and as a result might be lacking in his or her spiritual development. I ask my clients to imagine themselves helping a bed-ridden invalid who is cold and demands a blanket in an impatient and petulant tone of voice: would they be offended by the invalid's demand or tone, or would they understand that he is upset because he is incapable of getting anything without help?

I suggest that in fact they would feel thankful that they are able to move around and assist the invalid. Similarly, when your spouse is acting in an inferior manner, be thankful that you are not impaired in that way. Utilizing this view will help you to rise above such behavior by developing a sense of compassion and empathy for your spouse, which will strengthen your love for him or her. That love can eventually grow so great that, as it says in Proverbs (10:12), it "covers all flaws."[142]

The Write Way to Say "I Love You"

Many people find it difficult to speak lovingly to their spouse. This may be because one or both of you have grown accustomed to speaking in a certain impersonal or even hurtful manner. You may be afraid that an unexpectedly kind verbal overture may elicit a sarcastic or apathetic response, or it may be simply because words do not come easily to you. Consider writing a love letter to your spouse.

Writing allows you to chose your words carefully, and to have them heard in an unhurried, uninterrupted way. Additionally, the effort you take to sit down and write these loving sentiments indicates to your spouse, almost as much as the words themselves, that you care about him or her and your relationship.

These notes do not have to be long or overtly "mushy." Even little Post-its saying "I love you" or "Thank you for (whatever you are grateful for)" or a reference to a shared

142 *Zohar, Lech Lecha* 85b.

happy moment can go far in developing a warm and loving atmosphere.

Exercises And Meditations

Visualize yourself at the gym. See yourself being drawn to the weights. On the weights are written "compassion." As you lift them, your heart begins to pound and a flow of love begins to pulsate within you. You are stronger now. You are building compassion within yourself.

Consider how old hurts are affecting you now. Do challenges in your current relationships resemble hurts that occurred to you as a child? Acknowledge the pain of yesterday, then let it go. See yourself walking toward a body of water carrying two bags. Now you are standing at the water's edge and you open one bag. In this bag are all the hurts from your childhood. You do not need to hold onto that old pain. Affirm out loud, "I choose to let go of my past hurts. I am confident that I can remove my pains of yesterday. I want to have healthy relationships today." Take each negative emotion and throw it into the sea. Watch them all drift away. You feel a sense of release and relief.

Open the second bag and pull out positive emotions such as empathy, compassion, and forgiveness. You are filled with a sense of strength. You feel that you no longer need to protect yourself by withdrawing or growing angry. You feel able to relate to others in a more kind and loving manner.

Visualize yourself standing next to someone who has sinned against you. Focus on that person: see them standing before you, stuck in place, unable to move forward spiritually. Visualize the compassion spilling over from you to that person. See it releasing them to love G-d more freely and fully.

See yourself forgiving that person. Realize that your compassion has released their capacity to love. Your forgiveness has increased their ability to do *teshuvah*.

Sense the change in yourself for the better. Feel your greater dignity and the elevation of your soul.

During the recitation of the *Refa'ainu* prayer, pray to be healed of any past hurts and of any current negativity. Pray also for your spouse, or any person in your life to whom you are having difficulty relating.

Points For Practical Reflection

- Helping those closest to us is often a great challenge.

- Repay with kindness even someone who has offended you, especially family members.

- Forgiving your spouse is a vital aspect of maintaining peace in the home.

- Painful words may carry a message from Hashem.

- Forgiveness has many benefits.

- Empathy is the foundation of forgiveness.

- Be ready to apologize to your spouse, first and often.

- Praying for the refinement of your own character and that of your spouse is an effective aid in difficult times.

- Increasing your spirituality can be an effective aid to your relationship.

12

Model Communication

Your desire to walk in the ways of Hashem with your spouse may at times involve struggle. Be careful of the tactics you use to accomplish your goal, because the evil inclination is incredibly cunning at insinuating itself into such situations. The means you use to maintain and enhance the purity of your home should be refined and pleasant. Shlomo Hamelech/King Solomon said of the Torah (Proverbs 3:17), "Her ways are pleasant ways, and all her paths are peace." You cannot bring someone to a peaceful path if you yourself are not walking that path; you cannot have a positive influence on your spouse unless you yourself model appropriate behavior.

Paved With Good Intentions

Two Biblical stories teach how careful a person must be not to engage in thoughtless and wrong behavior, even when the goal is laudable.

The first story tells of Reuven's attempt to uphold the honor of his mother, Leah.

Yaakov was the father of the Twelve Tribes through four women: his two primary wives, Rachel and Leah, and two secondary wives, Bilhah (Rachel's maidservant) and Zilpah (Leah's maidservant). Yaakov loved Rachel best of all. After she died, Yaakov's eldest son Reuven assumed that Yaakov would choose Leah, his first wife, to take her place as his favorite. But to Reuven's horror, his father instead placed his bed next to that of Bilhah.

Rashi tells us that Reuven saw this as a humiliation of his mother. He therefore impetuously stormed into the tent and moved his father's bed. At that moment, it was decreed from heaven that Reuven would lose the ranks of kingship and priesthood that would ordinarily have gone to the first-born son.[143]

The Lubavitcher Rebbe explains[144] why Reuven suffered such drastic consequences for actions that stemmed from his desire to honor his mother. Reuven's character flaw is apparent from his father Yaakov's blessing to him (Genesis

---

143 Miller, Genesis, 1:349-351.

144 *Likkutei Sichos* vol 15 p. 439ff.

49:3-4): "Reuven, you are my first-born, my might, and the first-fruits of my strength; the excellency of dignity, and the excellency of power. [But you are] *unstable as water*, and you have not the excellency, because you went up to your father's bed; then you defiled it."

Reuven showed himself unsuited for a position of leadership in either the political or spiritual sphere. First, a king must have control over his emotions. When Reuven entered Bilhah's tent and moved his father's bed, he demonstrated that he was lacking in this essential quality. He should rather have said to himself, "I am shocked that my mother is not next in line. But if I move the bed, I will be dishonoring my father, who is a great *tzaddik* and whose wisdom is superior to mine. He undoubtedly has a reason for doing what he has done. Let me calm down and wait until later to discuss this matter with him."

Second, the High Priest represents the Jewish people and serves as an intermediary between them and Hashem. This position requires faith and subservience to G-d's will. In moving Yaakov's bed, Reuven displayed a lack of faith in Divine providence. When he saw his father's bed in Bilhah's tent, he should have realized and accepted that Hashem plans everything, and that it was not his place to second-guess his Heavenly father or his earthly father.

Act Responsibly

The severity of Reuven's punishment is all the more puzzling in light of the fact that when his younger brother Yehudah sinned egregiously, he was not punished at all. To the contrary, he was seemingly rewarded. To him, Yaakov stated (Genesis 49:10), "The scepter shall not depart from Yehudah, nor the ruler's staff from between his feet ... and unto him shall the obedience of the peoples be." Yehudah was given the kingship.

The episode in question involved Yehudah's daughter-in-law Tamar, who had been widowed of two of his sons. Seeing that Yehudah was not marrying her off to his third son, as he was obligated to do, she disguised herself as a harlot and succeeded in having Yehudah impregnate her while unaware of her true identity. When Tamar's pregnancy became visible, Yehudah convened a court and called for her to be executed. She did not want to humiliate Yehudah by making it known that he was the father. Therefore, she secretly sent him proof that he was the father and left the decision as to what to do up to him.

Yehudah faced a difficult choice: either let his daughter-in-law be executed or let himself be publicly humiliated. He could have allowed Tamar's execution to proceed and rationalized his silence by telling himself: "I have much holy work to accomplish, which will be destroyed if the community finds out."

Nevertheless, he did not take the easy way out. He knew that he was wrong for having denied his younger son to her. Instead of shielding his reputation, he took responsibility for his actions and saved Tamar from shame and death.

Why did Tamar seduce Yehudah? In Yaakov's blessing to his sons at the end of *Bereishis*, he tells Yehudah that the descendants of this union with Tamar will serve as the rulers of the Jewish people and that one of them would be the *Moshiach*. Our Sages explain[145] that Tamar had known this through the gift of prophecy.

But why should Yehudah be rewarded for an act that appears to have been rooted in passion rather than in holiness? Some commentators explain that Hashem deliberately overwhelmed Yehudah with an irresistible desire, in order to fulfill His Divine plan, (and his reward came for nobly putting Tamar's life before his honor).[146]

The Rebbe explains that the end result is what counts. Yehudah's act of acknowledging responsibility was the first step toward redemption, for Peretz, one of the twin sons born to him and Tamar, indeed became the forebearer of King David and ultimately, of the *Moshiach*.

In Reuven's case, by contrast, we see a missed opportunity. Here, the starting point seemed holy, but the

---

145 *Midrash Rabbah* to Gen. 38:18; *Sotah* 10b.

146 *Bereishis Rabba* 85:8, quoted on p. 211 of the *Stone Edition of the Chumash, Artscroll Series*, edited by Rabbi Nosson Scherman (New York: Mesorah Publications, Ltd., 1993).

end result was tragic. After sinning by moving his father's bed, Reuven was so brokenhearted that he spent the rest of his days in sackcloth and ashes. When the moment came that he could have saved his brother Yosef from the pit, Reuven was so preoccupied by his desire to do *teshuvah* that he ran to his father to ask forgiveness. In the meantime, Yosef was sold into slavery.

Reuven's act of neglecting responsibility was the first step leading to the exile of the Jewish people.

Wanting Is Not Enough

From these stories, we learn that whether or not one's original motive is holy is of little consequence if in the end, a person behaves in a manner contrary to holiness.

When you attempt to maintain and increase the holiness in your home, be careful not to not allow yourself to engage in any negative emotions or actions. If they do intrude, acknowledge them, remind yourself that they are wrong, stop them, and attempt to correct yourself.

Accept that you have work to do if you are to eradicate this behavior. A simple desire to change is not enough. It takes effort to maintain the holiness of your the initial intention and implement it in your daily life.

Strengthen Your Relationship

Do your utmost to deepen your marital bond. You can achieve this by being emotionally open, which means communicating your deepest thoughts and feelings with your spouse; by allowing yourself to be vulnerable with your spouse; and by sharing your love freely with your spouse, not withholding expressions of affection even when your spouse fails to live up to your expectations.

Upgrade the level of your communication. If T-Mobile and AT&T can upgrade, certainly Jewish couples can do so as well. (I once went to a cell phone outlet to replace a stolen cell phone and became very flustered when the salesperson repeatedly bombarded me with a sales pitch to upgrade my cell phone. All the while I kept thinking to myself, "I only want to upgrade my soul, Hashem. Please help me achieve this.")

When you work to improve communication with your partner, the ripple effect on your overall relationship is likely to bring dramatic rewards and most likely, sooner than you expect.

Be Calm

In the midst of a contentious moment, it is difficult to grasp the higher purpose of elevating one's soul to a more peaceful and unified state. You can mitigate feelings of pain and despondency by remembering that provocations with your spouse, child or other, are all meant to result in you being more patient, enduring, understanding and tolerant.

To prevent yourself from losing your equanimity when conflict with your spouse looms, engage in some positive thinking to help regain your inner strength and outer calm. No one gets it right all of the time. Perfecting relationships is a lifetime journey, one interaction at a time. It is all right if you do not have all of the solutions at your fingertips at every moment.

Remember the points made in Chapter 3 regarding silence. It is best to speak from a place of calmness. You will be heard better if you speak less, or at least if you speak less angrily.

If you have had a conflict with your spouse, do not confront him or her while you are still angry. Wait until your anger dissipates before bringing up your concerns. For the time being, you can remain silent—not as a way of punishing your spouse but in order to quiet the storm roiling within you until your equilibrium is restored.

This technique will help you pause mentally and emotionally so that you can keep your composure while in a pleasant tone of voice you say something like: "I hope you understand that I never meant to hurt you. Let's talk about this in a little while, when we're both feeling calmer."

Bring up the topic again when the atmosphere is calm. This will give each of you time to reflect on your behavior and its effects and to think about how you might have handled it differently.

Accept To Be Accepted

As we discussed in an earlier chapter, reciprocity is a major factor in a good relationship. Bear in mind that when you act more lovingly, that induces your spouse to respond in kind and to be more affectionate. Provide a model of the qualities of thoughtfulness, sensitivity, and generosity that you wish to see in your spouse. If you want to make your spouse feel comfortable in your presence, help him or her feel comfortable about him- or herself. When you are more accepting of your spouse, your spouse will grow to become more accepting of him- or herself and of you.

Presenting Your Feelings

If your negative thoughts about your spouse are so numerous that you do not know where to begin, ask yourself, "Which of these thoughts are worth bringing up for discussion?" If you limit yourself to your most essential concerns, you will feel less overwhelmed when initiating a conversation on this topic with your spouse. Your spouse in turn will not feel that he or she is being attacked on many fronts. You are also more likely to achieve some resolution on important issues if you deal with only one or two at a time.

Before you have that conversation, envision how you will discuss the situation, using empathetic, compassionate, and healing words rather than words that blame and moralize. Imagine how you would like to be spoken to if you were on the receiving end of this conversation.

Alternatively, imagine that you will be speaking to someone whose friendship you value and want to maintain. (People are usually very careful to avoid offending their friends. If they feel the need to reprove them, they do so as gently as possible—even if they themselves have been offended. If people had the same degree of consideration for their spouses as they display toward their friends, *Moshiach* would come sooner.)

Start the conversation with words of appreciation. You can either speak the simple truth, exaggerate to help boost your spouse's ego or, if you think it necessary, even engage in a "white lie."

That lays the groundwork for the next step, the more difficult task of presenting your complaint. Engage the "I" mode as you do so. For instance, "I know that right now I'm a little sensitive, but I feel it is important that you know that it really bothers me when …." And now you can express what has been bothering you.

The Discussion

While you are discussing these contentious issues, try to be aware of when you are allowing your ego to interfere with the resolution you are attempting to achieve. Pay attention to body signals that can warn you when you are about to lose control. For instance, before you raise your voice to yell, does your stomach tie itself into knots, does your nose flare, or does your face get hot? These signs are warning you to calm down.

If such signals occur during the discussion, close your eyes, take a deep breath and, if necessary, excuse yourself and walk away until you regain a measure of self-control. Then resume the conversation by thanking your spouse for giving you that personal time.

When there is either nothing else to say, or no more time in which to say it, review the major points that have been discussed. Share a moment of peace, and verbalize your feeling of resolution, for example, saying "I'm glad we talked" to reaffirm your bond once a decision has been reached.

Exercises and Meditations

Faced with a recurrent challenging situation, take the time to write down an inner dialogue with which you intend to combat your habitual responses to these upsetting situations.

After you have done that, at another calm moment, write down a dialogue between you and your spouse regarding the situation.

Visualize the goals you would like to achieve (e.g., the eradication of this situation) and the desired results of the conversation. Visualize your success in actualizing them. Realize that this may take considerable time.

Practice speaking in ways that you yourself would prefer to be spoken to. Put yourself in your spouse's place when you prepare your conversation.

Remember, "there is an eye that sees, an ear that hears, and a cellphone that records it all": Imagine that your conversation is being recorded and filmed and may go viral on social media. Imagine your reaction to such a circumstance.

Points For Practical Reflection

- You must model the behavior you wish to see in others.

- Pleasant ways will accomplish more than force.

- Improved communication leads to improved relationships.

- Do not respond in the heat of the moment.

- Address contentious issues when you are calm and prepared.

- Avoid overwhelming yourself or your spouse: prioritize and limit the number of issues to be addressed.

- Preface your discussion with words of appreciation for your spouse.

- End the discussion by expressing appreciation to your spouse for cooperating and sharing time with you.

13

Shalom Bayis and Parenting

The topic of child-rearing deserves a book of its own. However, it should be discussed here in brief with an emphasis on its connection to *shalom bayis*.

The Torah teaches us that no element of life is devoid of meaning and purpose, and that every interaction is divinely designed. Relationships are an important process that leads to completion (*shleimus*). We as human beings have a variety of emotions and personality styles that impact the way we think and feel about the people in our lives.

Our relationships have real and measurable consequences on our lives and those around us. The quality of our closest relationships profoundly affects how we feel about ourselves. The way we communicate both verbally and non-verbally affects the emotional, cognitive and physical development of our children, as well as our own physical and mental health.

Child-rearing is complex. Any parent can attest to the many rewards and equally distressing moments. Volumes of theories and practical approaches will not suffice to adequately explain parenting. Each child is a unique, dynamic individual who changes almost daily. For parents to properly guide their children, it is important to consider the environment that the parents create at home. I will primarily focus on the communication style between the adults, which is the template for the children's present and future relationships.

Rebbetzin Chanie Geisinsky, my *mashpia*, describes successful child-rearing as 50 percent consistent *chinuch* (Jewish education) and 50 percent *shalom bayis*. A healthy relationship between you and your spouse is critical to the success of every aspect of your child's healthy development, both physical and spiritual. Treating your spouse positively in front of your children is paramount. When husband and wife get along and demonstrate respect for each other, it helps the children get along better, and also lays a foundation for children to respect their parents.

It is acceptable to occasionally express disagreements amicably in front of children. Couples should definitely discuss many issues in the presence of their children. It teaches the children how relationships work. However, never let your children hear the two of you argue in a state of rage or anger; this is toxic! Seeing parents in such a state makes children feel terrified, unsafe, and heartbroken. In addition, when one parent yells and shames the other parent, the children witnessing these events feel ashamed as well.

Our Sages teach that the greatest suffering is shame, and this is especially true in the case of children. Shame may cause a child such distress that eventually his life becomes unbearable and he may have little energy to achieve his potential. Even when one spouse may think the other needs to improve his or her communication, they should refrain from criticizing the other. It is better for a child to receive some overly strict discipline than to see parents fighting over this issue. Instead, after such an episode, when the spouse is not present, tell the children, "Tatty/Mommy may speak very strongly to you, but know that we both love you and mean well."

Rabbi Shlomo Carlebach taught that according to the *Zohar*, when Hashem said, "Do not commit murder,"[147] the ordinary Jew heard just that. A Jew on a higher level heard Hashem saying, "Do not embarrass anyone in public." Someone who was on an even higher level heard Hashem saying, "Do not take your anger out on anyone." And a person who was on the highest level heard Hashem saying, "Do not ignore anyone." [148]

147 *Exodus* 20:13.

148 E-mail communication from Reb Sholom Brodt, teacher at Yeshivat Simchat Shlomo in Jerusalem, March 18, 2012.

Applying this to parenting, it could be added: do not embarrass your children, do not take your anger out on your children, and do not ignore the outcries of your children, even if you feel consumed by your suffering within a painful marriage.

When the situation has calmed down, the parents can work together on reducing the amount of stress in the home, making the other aware when they speak aggressively or act tense. For instance, a parent may say, "I think that we can both work on decreasing the stress in this home. Let's help each other act more calmly in front of the children, especially when we have to discipline them." By preparing a strategy in advance, a person can prevent many conflicts. If you cannot come up with an amicable solution, ask the advice of a Rav or a spiritual advisor who knows your spouse.

New research has revealed that exposure to common family problems during childhood and early adolescence affects brain development, which could lead to mental health issues in later life.

The study led by Dr. Nicholas Walsh, lecturer in developmental psychology at the University of East Anglia, used brain imaging technology to scan teenagers aged 17-19. He found that those who experienced mild to moderate family difficulties between birth and 11 years of age had developed a smaller cerebellum, an area of the brain associated with skill learning, stress regulation and sensory-motor control. The researchers also suggest that a smaller cerebellum may be a risk indicator of psychiatric disease later in life, as it is consistently found to be smaller in virtually all psychiatric illnesses.

Dr. Walsh said: "These findings are important because exposure to adversities in childhood and adolescence is the biggest risk factor for later psychiatric disease." Also, psychiatric illnesses are a huge public health problem and the biggest cause of disability in the world.

Fighting is an indication that your communication isn't working. When one or both parents are tired or stressed, an occasional dispute is understandable. However, ongoing conflicts are cause for concern and need to be addressed seriously.

A teacher moved to a town and began giving a shiur, which quickly became popular. One of the established teachers thought that the teachings were cultish, so he slandered the new teacher and urged people not to attend his shiur. One rainy day, as this teacher was walking down the street, he saw the new teacher slip and fall in the mud. The teacher hurried over to him. He bent down as if to help the fallen man, but instead picked up some mud and threw it at him, hissing disgustedly: "You deserve it!" then he walked off.

The new teacher got up and ran after the other man. "Wait, teacher, please!" he called out. The teacher continued walking, but the mud-stained teacher called out again: "Please wait!" The teacher slowed down slightly. "Please, teacher," the new teacher gasped, "please, accept my apologies. I do not know exactly how I have hurt you, but the pain I caused you must have been great for you to hate me." Both men stopped walking.

The new teacher asked humbly: "Please tell me, what I have done to you? I must know so that I can do teshuvah properly."

The other teacher was taken aback. For a moment, he doubted the new teacher's sincerity, but searching the man's mud-streaked face, he saw only true humility. Astonished and ashamed, he thought to himself: "This is a G-dly man before me!" He embraced the new teacher and said, "It is I who must do teshuvah." After that, the relationship between the two men improved. They began studying together and became close friends.

This sort of self-reflection is especially important in regard to your relationship with your children. When they behave disrespectfully to you, stop and think to yourself: "What have I done to cause them to be in this mood?"

There is a second lesson to glean from this story. Every day children are under pressure from parents, teachers, bus drivers and siblings. They "fall in the mud" many times over the course of the day. When your children come home, consider that they may have had many "muddy moments" before coming through your door. Treat them with compassion. Do your best to help them feel better. At the very least, do not throw more mud at them.

Exercises and Meditations

Picture yourself remaining calm in front of your family even when you feel like indulging in an emotional outburst. Concentrate on how precious your family is to you, until you can control the impulse to act unkindly towards them.

Repeat the following affirmations throughout the day, even before a challenging situation arises:

"I want to unite, not to win."

"I want peace, not victory."

"Making peace is the greatest victory."

"My goal is to give peace of mind, not *pieces* of my mind."

"*Shalom bayis* is the surest path to raising emotionally healthy children."

"My efforts to become a positive role model will maximize my success as a parent."

Plan to avoid fighting in front of the child(ren). If you think you might give in to your urge to fight, turn around and walk away. Recognize that when you don't walk away, you are putting your need to vent ahead of your children's well-being and peace of mind.

After you walk away, write down all your thoughts and feelings on the situation, so you can discuss it later when the children aren't around.

Have your discussion somewhere private, with minimal distractions and interruptions. Deal with your spouse closely and personally. Express your needs to your partner calmly and clearly. Be specific; he or she may not know what those needs are.

Work out the problem with cooperation, not competition.

Points for Practical Reflection

- Your family members are the most precious part of your life.

- Raising your voice in anger, speaking sarcastically, or otherwise belittling your spouse or children is very damaging to *shalom bayis* and to the emotional health of your family.

- A parent must model the qualities of thoughtfulness, sensitivity, and generosity that will set the standards for the children.

- Consider that if your children treat you disrespectfully, you may have done something to warrant that.

- Children experience many difficult moments throughout their day; make your home a place of happy moments for them.

- Professional counseling that is sensitive to Torah ethics and values may be useful in helping you achieve healthier perspectives on your marriage.

14

Gratitude and Patience

The Alter Rebbe explains that the *Haftorah* of *Shabbos Shira* (when the story of the Exodus from Egypt is read in the synagogue) is the Song of Devorah, to teach us that all salvation comes because of the righteous deeds of women. When the Jewish people left Egypt, the waters of the Red Sea/Sea of Reeds split, allowing them to cross on dry land. To celebrate that miraculous event, both the men and the women, separately, sang a song of praise to G-d.

The women, however, accompanied their song with cymbals and dancing, manifesting a higher level of joy than did the men. This musical accompaniment was especially praiseworthy because the forethought the women demonstrated by bringing along their instruments indicated that they were secure in the belief that G-d would save them, and that they would need these instruments to celebrate that salvation.[149]

"With All Your Might"

No matter what you are going through, no matter what mood you may find yourself in, recognize that all events are orchestrated by Hashem, Who is compassionate and Who alone knows what is best for you. It is for us to thank and praise G-d for all that He does for us, whether or not we can clearly understand how it is for our benefit.

This idea is alluded to by Psalms 150:

Hallelukah, Praise the L-rd!

Praise G-d in His Holiness.

Praise Him in the firmament of His strength.

Praise Him for His mighty acts.

Praise Him according to His abundant greatness.

Praise Him with the call of the shofar;

---

149 *Likkutei Dibburim*. King David learned this from the women, as we see that when the time came to bring the Ark back to Jerusalem, he "and all the house of Israel played before the LORD with all manner of instruments made of cypress-wood, and with harps, and with psalteries, and with timbrels, and with sistra, and with cymbals." (2 *Samuel* 6:15)

Praise Him with a harp and lyre.

Praise Him with timbrel and dance;

Praise Him with stringed instruments and flute.

Praise Him with resounding cymbals;

Praise Him with clanging cymbals;

Let every soul praise the L-rd.

Praise the L-rd.

The Radak (Rabbi David Kimchi, 1160–1235, biblical commentator, philosopher, and grammarian) points out that the root word *hallel*, "praise," appears thirteen times in this psalm, alluding to G-d's Thirteen Attributes of Mercy.[150] Radak states that "the Psalmist begins to enumerate nine different musical instruments, each of which produces a different sound. He exhorts man to praise G-d in many ways with every type of musical accompaniment."[151]

There are happy-sounding instruments and others that are more subdued. [152]Each instrument represents a different state in a person's life.

---

150 "The Lord! The Lord! G-d, Compassionate and Gracious, Slow to anger and Abundant in Kindness and Truth, Preserver of kindness for thousands of generations, Forgiver of iniquity, willful sin, and error, and Who Cleanses (but does not cleanse completely, recalling the iniquity of parents upon children and grandchildren, to the third and fourth generations)" *Exodus* 34:6-7.

151 Rabbi Avraham Chaim Feuer, *Tehillim*, ArtScroll Tanach Series vol. 2 page 1736-1740, footnote 1.

152 The Sages give varying descriptions of these instruments. Some of the commentaries believe that the nine consisted of a *shofar*, *neivel* (10-stringed

For example, Rabbi Moshe Cordovero explains[153] that the powerful blast of the *shofar* teaches that even when a person finds himself in a crisis and trembles with fear, he should remember that at that moment he is still the beneficiary of G-d's abundant mercy.

The harp is a delicate instrument that produces soft, soothing sounds. This represents serene periods of life, when a person has the peace of mind to meditate on the greatness of Hashem's kindness.

The timbrel produces loud, exciting sounds. These represent the hustle-and-bustle of life. Pressure is constant, and a person rushes around in a frenzy. Despite the relentless demands on his time, he must set aside time on a daily basis to praise Hashem for guiding all events and human affairs.

The flute produces a mournful, haunting sound, representing those times in life when a person is filled with fear or sadness.

In his explanation of the final verse, "Let all souls praise," the Radak states that "having enumerated the many different instruments and musical tones with which one may praise G-d, the Psalmist concludes that nothing can compare with the praise the soul can offer to G-d. For the intelligent soul utilizes every human sense to discover the

---

instrument), *kinor* (harp), *tof* (timbrel or tambourine), *machol*, (flute), *minim* (either a type of flute or organ), *ugav*, (another type of flute), *tziltzelai shema*, (cymbals), and *tziltzelai teruah* (trumpets).

153 Feuer, *Tehillim*, 2:1738.

wonders of G-d's creation and to appreciate G-d's abundant kindness." And he concludes: "Far greater than the most sublime instrumental song of praise is the song of the human soul that utilizes its full potential in His service."[154]

Last but Not Least, Gratitude

Counting one's blessings is a vital ingredient in a good life. Therefore, even if your relationship with your spouse is threadbare, work to appreciate what good there is in it. Just having a partner with whom to share your life is reason enough to feel grateful.

Cultivate a healthy perspective and an attitude of gratitude; these will allow a feeling of security to develop within you, which you will be empowered to share with your partner. This sharing in itself will contribute to peace and harmony in the home.

An associated key to handling the challenges of life and enhancing your relationship with your spouse is to develop and strengthen your faith and trust in G-d. As you increasingly recognize G-d's omniscient and beneficent day-to-day involvement in your life, you develop greater resilience and more serenity in the face of life's inevitable vicissitudes—including the challenges of marriage.

154 Ibid.

Develop the habit of constantly reminding yourself that everything you are encountering—including the difficulties in your relationship with your spouse—comes from Hashem with the purpose of helping you grow.

Pray to G-d and firmly believe that your prayers will not go unanswered. Although the answer may not always be the one you would have chosen, trust that that G-d, Who is both benevolent and omniscient, has orchestrated the event with His wisdom and compassion and designed it ultimately in your best interest.

Never Stop Working on Your Self-Improvement

Our Sages[155] teach that a person ought to engage in *teshuvah* throughout his life.

As the Ramban writes in his famous letter of ethical instruction to his son: "Review your actions every morning and evening, and in this way live all your days in repentance."[156]

King David, in *Tehillim* (chapter 55, verse 17) tells us that "The sacrifices of G-d are a broken spirit; a broken and a contrite heart, O G-d, Thou wilt not despise." The Alter

---

155 *Shabbat* 153a.

156 *Iggeres HaRamban*, Feuer p. 20.

Rebbe writes[157]: "The true humbling of the heart, so that it be broken and crushed, so that the spirit of impurity and the Side of Evil will be removed, is achieved through being a 'master of accounting' with all the profundity of one's mind." We should scrutinize our behavior and motives with the same degree of attention to detail that a businessman dedicates to examining his business ledger and accounting for every cent.

Daily *teshuvah* goes a long way to fostering humility, which, as we discussed earlier, is key to creating a harmonious relationship.

The Date Palm

In this book, my goal has been to help you build a harmonious and joyful relationship with your spouse. I have stressed that the best way to do that is to strengthen your relationship with G-d, through a growing appreciation of His love for you and His plan for you. That strength will help you motivate yourself to work on refining your character, which in turn will lead you to achieve a fulfilling marriage.

Now that you are coming to the end of this book, give it to your spouse to read. Review it regularly by yourself, and perhaps, occasionally with your spouse. My hope is that you will take its messages to heart until they become a part of

157 Wineberg, *Iggeres HaTeshuvah* of *Tanya* vol. 3, page 1076.

you. If you feel that you need further assistance, I am always available to help you with individualized counseling.

I would like to leave you with one more thought to help you persevere in your journey to marital fulfillment. If you find that you are not seeing the results that you seek in your relationship, don't lose hope. To those who were on the verge of giving up on their efforts, the Lubavitcher Rebbe provided the example of the date palm: although it takes up to 70 years to mature, its dates are among the sweetest of all fruits.

My blessing to you, dear reader, is that you too will taste the sweetness of a healthy, happy, mature marriage and that you will reach new heights through kindness in marriage.

Getting Ready for Redemption

The Lubavitcher Rebbe states[158] that the prolonged suffering of the Jewish people during their nearly 2,000-year exile from the land of Israel constituted an atonement for the sin of baseless hatred, which was the root cause of the destruction of the *Bais HaMikdash*. At this point in time, we have rectified that sin. Now our task is simply to dress ourselves in "garments" of fine character traits and good deeds.[159] The more a person refines himself, the

158 *Likkutei Sichos*, 27:297; *Toras Menachem*, 1982, 3:1226.

159 See Appendix.

more his G-dly soul is revealed, and the greater will be his appreciation of G-dliness when *Moshiach* arrives.

This may be illustrated by the following parable:

There were once two brothers who for years refused to speak to each other. Their father passed away shortly before one of the brothers was to marry off his eldest daughter.

The deceased father appeared in a dream to this brother and begged him to end the feud and invite the other brother to the wedding. When this brother awoke, he felt remorse for the strained relationship between himself and his brother, and sent him an invitation.

When the other brother received the invitation, he thought to himself: "My brother must be crazy! Does he really imagine that after everything he did to me, I will attend the wedding as if everything is forgiven? He can forget it; I'm not coming!" He tossed the invitation away and tried to put it out of his mind. Deep down, however, he felt conflicted. When the wedding day arrived, he was so distressed that he put on his pajamas early in the evening to ensure he would not surrender to any desire to go, and he crawled into bed.

Meanwhile, the wedding was taking place amid great joy. Yet the gladness felt by the father of the bride was diminished by the absence of his brother. One of the fiddlers noticed that he seemed downcast and distracted, and asked him if something was wrong. The man confided his dilemma to the fiddler.

The fiddler responded, "Tell me where your brother lives. I will go to his home and bring him here." After receiving the address, he left.

When the fiddler arrived at the brother's house, he stood outside the window and began playing his fiddle. The brother, tossing and turning in bed, heard the sweet sound of music. He opened the window and became so enraptured by the music that he went outside in his pajamas to listen.

The fiddler motioned to the brother to follow him, and, as if in a trance, the brother complied. They reached the wedding hall, and before the brother realized what had happened, he was inside amid the celebration.

The bride's father spotted him and immediately ran to embrace him. After they shared the happiness of their reunion, the father of the bride said, "How good it is to see you. But why did you come to the wedding wearing pajamas?"

What Are You Wearing?

Like the wedding in this story, the redemption will be a special moment between G-d and Israel. We will all be invited to the ultimate wedding, when Moshiach comes. But how will we be dressed: in pajamas, or in beautiful garments of kindness and the love of our fellow-Jew?

Every kind act beautifies us. Every kind act to our spouse also completes us. Every step across the bridge of kindness brings us closer to our spouse, closer to Moshiach, and closer to G-d and thus reach new heights.

Exercises and Meditations

When you say *Modeh Ani* ("I thank You") in the morning, think of all the good in your life for which you can feel grateful to G-d: the parts of your body that are healthy and functioning; a roof over your head; the people you share your life with; your abilities and talents and the opportunities to use them.

At a quiet time of the day, sit down and make a detailed list of other items that you can add to your *Modeh Ani* meditation.

Note the areas in your marital relationship in which you think you still need to improve. Pick one aspect to work on for three weeks (bearing in mind the thought that a habit takes at least that long to break—recall the personal example given earlier). If, for example, you resolve to maintain a pleasant tone of voice when communicating with your spouse, practice speaking in that tone when you are alone. Write out possible responses to comments by your spouse on topics you think are likely to arise.

Reward yourself for having come this far, and for every additional step you take.

Reward your spouse, too.

Points For Practical Reflection

- Remember G-d is orchestrating your life.

- Try to maintain a healthy perspective.

- Perspective makes it easy to cultivate an attitude of gratitude.

- Gratitude leads to a feeling of security.

- Emotional security brings peace and harmony to a home.

- Reviewing your actions daily leads to repentance, repentance leads to humility, humility leads to harmony.

- To strengthen your relationship with your spouse, strengthen your relationship with G-d.

- Achieving good things takes time.

- When Moshiach comes, it will be better to be dressed in garments of good deeds than in pajamas.

- Every kind deed is another step on the bridge of kindness.

Improve Your Character by Learning *Chassidus*

I learned from my own personal journey toward spiritual development that regular study of *Chassidus* is essential for true transformation. As far back as I can remember, I always had a constant yearning to gain mastery over the "not-so-positive" me. Nevertheless all of my determination to succeed and my feelings of closeness to Hashem were not enough to subdue my animal soul. Only through the study of *Chassidus* did I acquire the tools, mainly deep meditative prayer, to begin the process of transforming my animal soul and unlocking the G-dly soul within me. Although change was very gradual, I finally began to see real progress.

The teachings of *Chassidus* help us make our animal soul a true partner with our G-dly soul. As such, studying *Chassidus* and deep meditative prayer are the most effective way of cleansing ourselves of our negative tendencies. The Lubavitcher Rebbe teaches us that "learning Torah is a spice to sweeten the *yetzer hara* into a *yetzer hatov.*"[160]

According to the Lubavitcher Rebbe, our generation needs these teachings more than previous generations, for with them we prepare ourselves for the imminent arrival of the *Moshiach.*

The Torah comprises three revealed aspects— *peshat* (simple meaning), *remez* (allusions) and *derush*

160 Cf. Chapter 2.

(homiletics)—as well as one concealed aspect, called *sod* (secrets). *Chassidus* is a new channel of spiritual life force that reveals the esoteric aspect of the Torah. It guides a person on how to act beyond the letter of the law, and helps him transform his character as a result of reaching his highest spiritual root (called the "*yechidah* of his *neshamah*"). It also helps a person improve the world at large by arousing the world from its spiritual unconsciousness and giving it a new life-force.[161]

Once the Rebbe Maharash asked his father, the Tzemach Tzedek, "What did our grandfather (the Alter Rebbe) want to achieve with the ways of *Chassidus* and the study of *Chassidus*?"

The Tzemach Tzedek answered: "[The goal of] the ways of Chassidus is that all Chassidim should be like one family, [united] in love according to the Torah. Chassidus is vitality, bringing energy and light into everything, even into those things that are undesirable. We should recognize our own evil as it is, so that we can correct it."[162]

In practical terms, look for ways to infuse your life with spiritual energy by learning Chassidus regularly—in a local class or, if that is not possible, by phone, e-mail, the Internet, CDs or MP3 recordings.

161 Rabbi Menachem Mendel Schneerson, *The Essence of Chassidus* (New York: Kehot Publication Society, 2003), p. 44.

162 *HaYom Yom*, 24 Teves, page 24.

Learning Chassidus can contribute to the wellbeing of your marriage, for several reasons.

First, when you learn Chassidus, you develop a closer relationship with G-d that develops into an intense love for Him. That love refines your character traits, and in consequence you treat your spouse with greater compassion and acceptance. Once you are happier with yourself, the things that you found annoying about your spouse will cease to be as bothersome.

This change in perspective can be illustrated by the following story:

A poor woman parked her car on the street. She could barely afford the quarter for the parking meter. To her chagrin, she returned to the car a few minutes late, to find a $150 ticket stuck to her windshield. Needless to say, she felt terrible.

A week later, she won $50 million in the lottery. Again, she parked her car, deposited a quarter in the parking meter and returned to find another $150 ticket. But this time, the second ticket did not upset her. In fact, she smiled as she looked at it, because it reminded her of the change in her status and helped her feel that much more grateful.

When you realize what greatness you have gained, the thorns that pricked you along the way are overshadowed by the roses.

Appendix A: Animal Soul, G-dly Soul and Garments of the Soul

There is a popular and persistent misconception—arising most probably from the related but separate topic of the dual and dueling human *yotzros*, inclinations—that the soul is split between good and bad. This is an incorrect oversimplification. As discussed briefly in Chapter One, the human soul actually has five levels. Two of these are really beyond our comprehension. The other three relate to our daily lives.

In relation to these three soul levels, the *Tanya* teaches that every Jew possesses an animal soul and a G-dly soul.

(The third is not germane to this discussion.) Both are holy, and both are necessary to serving G-d.

The animal soul, associated with the left side of the human body, corresponds to a person's bodily nature and is likened to a "wild ox." It is an untamed, extremely powerful force that actually emanates from a very high plane of existence. The G-dly soul, which is associated with the right side of the human body, emanates from a somewhat lower existential plane, and needs to harness the animal soul in order to direct it and use its power to reach higher levels of spirituality (*Likutei Torah, Adam Ki Yakriv*).

All Jews possess an innate drive to integrate the disparate elements within themselves, to make themselves whole and reflect a seamless internal consistency that is powered by the animal soul, yet shaped and directed by the G-dly soul.

As Jews, we have been blessed by G-d with a gift of infinite value that provides us with the tools we need to accomplish this. That gift is the Torah. Torah study and the performance of its 613 mitzvos bring a holy consistency to our thoughts, speech, and actions. This leads to oneness with our Creator, which is the fulfillment of our mission on earth.

By doing *mitzvos*, we open ourselves up to the light of G-d. This occurs via the agency of the *Shechinah*, which is "the intermediary between the upper and the lower worlds. It receives its holiness from Hashem and transmits it below."[163] The Alter Rebbe teaches that "the worlds cannot endure or receive the light of the *Shechinah*, that it might actually dwell and enclothe itself in them, without a 'garment' to screen and conceal its light from them, so that they may not become entirely nullified."[164]

The physical protection conferred by doing a mitzvah or a good deed is alluded to by the verse, "Charity protects from death." The spiritual protection conferred is alluded to by our Sages' statement (*Sotah* 3a) that a person does not sin unless a spirit of folly enters him. This is because when we perform *mitzvos* we are less susceptible to succumbing to folly, and then we do not come to sin.

The essence of a Jew's lofty soul is revealed by his or her thoughts, speech, and actions. A person's thoughts are his internal reality, whereas his speech and action are his external realities, the face he presents to the world. In Chassidic philosophy, our thoughts, speech, and actions are called the *levushim* ("garments") of the G-dly soul. Just as garments adorn a person, the spiritual garments of Torah and mitzvos beautify those who "wear" them. As clothing protects the wearer from the elements, so too *mitzvos* and Torah study protect a person from falling prey to the distorted thinking that leads to sin. And, just as sunglasses shade a person's eyes, enabling them to adjust to the outdoor light and enjoy the landscape, so too *mitzvos* enable human beings to perceive the Divine radiance without being

163 Rabbi DovBer Pinson, *Reincarnation and Judaism: The Journey of the Soul* (New Jersey: Jason Aronson, Inc., 1999), p. 8.

164 *Lessons in Tanya, Likkutei Amarim* ,vol. 2, p. 788 .

blinded. Without *mitzvos* as an intermediary, a person would be unable to handle the intensity of G-d's holy emanations, or *sefiros* (faculties).[165]

Mitzvos, Torah study, and acts of kindness protect us by acting as a shield against the evil spirit, and they beautify us as garments of the G-dly soul. They allow the G-dly radiance to dwell inside us without destroying us, and also allow our specific G-dly emanations to shine.[166]

Our faculties express themselves through our physicality, so when we perform *mitzvos* physically, our G-dly energy is to be channeled into this world. Heaven and earth are both in us, so we become mediators, or interpreters, between the two. No other creation on earth can do this.

Chassidus explains the mechanism behind this as follows.

Sefiros are the ten G-dly qualities, "ethereal spiritual realities through which Hashem can be seen in this world....They can't really be understood intellectually, only experientially," according to Rabbi David Aaron. In his book, *Seeing God*, Rabbi Aaron compares trying to define *sefiros* with trying to define the difference between chocolate

---

165 Without the mediating and moderating effects of the *mitzvos* to enable us to receive the Divine emanations, we too would be as vulnerable as the crystal goblet beneath Niagara falls. Mental and emotional problems begin when there is too much light and too little vessel, that is, not enough prayer, meditation, and Torah learning.

166 See my book *Reaching New Heights through Prayer and Meditation*.

and vanilla to someone who hasn't tasted both flavors. [167] It's impossible to describe unless you have actually tasted them. *Kabbalah* teaches us that there are ten qualities that make up reality and that each one is like a different color in the spectrum of Divine light. Through them, the soul can see and begin to understand the infinite and incomprehensible reality that is Hashem.

The essence of a Jew's lofty soul is revealed by his or her holy thoughts, words and actions, which correspond to the first three *sefiros*, the soul's three instruments of expression[168]: *Chochmah, Binah*, and *Da'as. Chochmah* means "wisdom" or "intellectual awareness," the sparking, intuitive flash of illumination that is the beginning of intellectual revelation. *Binah* is "understanding" or "comprehension," the deep contemplation of a subject which crystallizes and clarifies the details of the idea that was absorbed in *Chochmah. Da'as* is "knowledge," the ability to assimilate wisdom and information in order to develop healthy emotions and change one's behavior.

Together, these three *sefiros* are referred to by the acronym *ChaBaD*. Mitzvos are comparable to garments in that they can be donned or shed at will. Imagine a beggar clothed in nothing but rags. If the beggar's garments were exchanged with the royal garments of a king, it is not likely that the beggar would be recognized. Conversely, let us imagine a king who is stripped of his crown and royal attire

---

167 Rabbi David Aaron, *Seeing G-d: Ten Life-Changing Lessons of Kabbalah* (USA: Penguin Group Inc., 2000) pp. 45-47.

168 *Tanya*, Chapter 4, pg. 74.

and forced to wear a beggar's clothing. It is obvious that he would not be treated with the deference to which he is accustomed.

Thus, when the soul utilizes any of these three powers, it is said to be clothed in them; when it does not use them, it is said to be divested of them.[169] Just as fine garments give expression to the wearer's beauty and importance, so do these garments give expression to the soul's faculties of intellect and emotion.[170]

Rabbi Wineberg elucidates:

It is through the mitzvos we do that our souls are able to achieve ever-higher levels. The Alter Rebbe compares the 248 positive mitzvos to the 248 organs in the human body. Just as the organs give expression to the faculties, i.e., the soul faculty of sight is expressed through the organ of the eyes, so too each mitzvah is an appropriate vessel for the specific emanation of the Divine will that desires the Jew to perform the particular commandment.

At some point, though the analogy between literal garments and the "garments" of the soul breaks down.[171]

The Alter Rebbe states that, unlike physical garments, which are less important than their wearer, the garments of the Divine soul are even loftier than the soul which

---

169 Ibid.

170 Ibid.

171 Lessons in *Tanya*, vol. 2 *Likkutei Amarim*, chap. 46, page 689; vol. 1, chapter 4, p. 79.

"wears" them. Thus wearing its garments—i.e. thinking and speaking words of Torah and acting in performance of the commandments—elevates the soul to a higher level. For, since Torah and the commandments are one with G-d, the Jew, by donning the garments of Torah and the commandments, also becomes united with Him.

Below *ChaBaD* are character traits, or *middos*, of which there are seven, and which man should strive to embody: *Chesed*, the quality of giving and of attraction to G-dliness; *Gevurah*, strength, self-restraint against the temptations offered by the *yetzer hara*; *Tiferes*, beauty, harmony; *Netzach*, victory, overcoming barriers; *Hod*, self-nullification, giving space to others; *Yesod*, foundation, a balance between *Netzach* and *Hod*, and *Malchus*, kingship, dignity and confidence in oneself, with all *sefiros* in perfect harmony.

G-d created the world with *Chochmah*, which is pure and unadulterated, and close to the truth of existence—meaning, to G-d's light. As Hashem created increasingly physical worlds, He increasingly hid this light. The further along this process of descent, the more do evil *klippos* (sing. *klippah*), or "shells," conceal this light. Although these intellectual qualities and character traits can be used for holy purposes, they can be used to pernicious ends. In the latter case, they are grasped by the *klippos*.

The Alter Rebbe writes that the "evil of *klippah* is stronger in the *middos* than in [*ChaBaD*,] the intellectual faculties, since on that level (of *middos*) [the *klippos*] draw more vitality from holiness than they do on the level of

ChaBad. [172] Because "the evil of *ChaBaD*" is relatively minor, it "can be transformed" to good through intensive Torah study.

Appendix B: Guided Imagery

The Tzemach Tzedek famously said, "Think good, and it will be good." For those of us who are not on the level of such a *tzaddik*, it is often difficult to "think good" when we are in a situation that is causing us pain. Certain techniques can be very helpful in achieving the mental state that will allow us to break out of harmful habituated thought processes. When we can actively direct our thoughts in a positive direction, our situation will "be good."

In his writings regarding the necessity and rewards of meditation, the Lubavitcher Rebbe pointed out that meditation was an aid to "psychological health and peace of mind."

The concept of tzimtzum, "contraction," is illustrated by the example of mirrors, which may be large or small. The image reflected in the small mirror represents the object in all its details, except in the diminutive form. The naked eye requires aids to see small objects. The "eye" of the intellect likewise requires "aids" to apprehend subtle concepts, namely the power of cognition. In a somewhat analogous way, it can be conceived that the act of tzimtzum has not essentially changed anything except [that it has become] greatly "contracted," as in the example of the small mirror. It is therefore more difficult to see the G-dliness that is everywhere as it is before tzimtzum, and consequently an "aid" is necessary, namely hisbonenus, "contemplation" (Letters from the Rebbe, vol. 2, page 37).

The Rebbe cautioned that since meditation was so helpful and so powerful, it held great potential for misuse or abuse. He warned that it was essential that "kosher" paths to and forms of meditation be publicized, in order that people would be able to benefit from it without being hurt.

The Rebbe clarified this concern in the following words:

There is an issue, which is connected with the physical and psychological health of many Jews, that demands attention. It is quite possible that these words will have no effect. Nevertheless, the health of a Jew is such an important matter, that efforts should be made even when there is not a sure chance of success.

This issue is the idea of meditation. Meditation has its roots in the very beginning of the Jewish heritage. The Torah commentaries explain that Avraham and the other Patriarchs chose to be shepherds so that they could spend their time in solitude.

Their lives were not simple, physical lives. On the contrary, they were totally given over to the service of G-d to the point where they were called "G-d's chariot." [That metaphor was chosen because just as a chariot has no will of its own and is totally controlled by its driver, similarly their lives were totally controlled by G-d.]

They chose a profession that would allow them to live such a spiritual existence. Therefore, they became shepherds, spending their days in the fields, in solitude, rather than becoming involved in the hubbub of life in the cities.

The same holds true today. There are certain aspects of psychological health and tranquility that can be attained by taking oneself out of contact with the surrounding hullabaloo and tumult of life.

By retreating into solitude, (not necessarily leaving the city,) and by withdrawing into seclusion for a period of time, one may attain psychological health and peace of mind. This manner of behavior strengthens the individual and guards his mental health.

This process involves withdrawing from the clamor and tumult of the street and meditating on an object that brings about serenity and peace of mind.

The Torah's statement (Devarim 30:15), "Behold I have set before you life and goodness, death and evil" is applicable to all matters. Every aspect of life can be utilized for the good or for the opposite.

For example, the sun, moon, and stars are necessary for life to exist on earth, bringing about a multitude of good. However, these celestial bodies have also been worshipped as deities.

One may ask (as the Talmud does [Avodah Zarah 54b]): "Since these celestial bodies have been worshipped as false deities, shouldn't they be destroyed?" The Talmud's answer is most instructive: "Should the world be destroyed because of these fools?!"

The same applies with regard to meditation. Though essentially positive, meditation can also be used in a destructive manner. There are those who have connected meditation to actually bowing down to an idol or to a man and worshipping it or him, offering incense before them, and so on.

These cults have spread throughout the United States and throughout Eretz Yisrael as well. Some of these cults have been called by a refined name, "transcendental-meditation," thereby implying that it is something above limits, above our limited intellect.

However, they have also incorporated into their practices the offering of incense and other actions that clearly come under the heading of idolatry.

Since we are living in the darkness of Exile, many Jewish youth have fallen into this snare. Before they become involved with this cult, they were troubled and disturbed; the cult was able to relate to them and offer them peace of mind.

However, their form of meditation is connected with idolatry: burning incense, bowing down to a Guru, etc. Since these idolatrous aspects are not publicized, there are those who have not raised their voices in protest.

Moreover, they are unsure if such a protest would be met with success, and since no one has asked for their opinion, they think to themselves why protest and enmesh oneself in a questionable situation.

However, while those who should be protesting remain silent, Jewish youth are becoming involved in idolatry, a sin so severe that the Torah declares that one should sacrifice his life rather than worship idols. Moreover, this scourge is spreading, ensnaring youth and adults alike.

Additionally, since "One sin leads to another," even those who are not yet involved in the more severe and more clearly idolatrous forms of this group will eventually be drawn into this aspect of idolatry, in their search of a "holier" and more "sacred" Guru-deity.

A program must therefore be organized to spread "kosher meditation." While there are those who argue against this, maintaining that "kosher meditation" might well lead to "non-kosher meditation," the fact of the matter is that this is not so.

It is opposite the spirit of Judaism and especially opposite the spirit of Chassidus to withhold assistance from anyone in need of it....

("Kosher Meditation", from the pamphlet *Mental Health*, pp. 5-9.)

Elsewhere, the Rebbe wrote:

*The manner of meditation required by all is that which
is part and parcel of one's spiritual service. Thus we find
the directive in the Shulchan Aruch that prior to prayer an
individual should meditate on G-d's greatness and man's
insignificance. This meditation, however, is one that has fixed
times – prior to prayer – and specific goals, and not [simply] the
calming of one's nerves. The second crucial feature is that the
meditation must be based on a kosher idea or Torah concept,
e.g., "Shema Yisrael," and the concepts implied therein. This will
lead the individual to a greater awareness of G-d's greatness
and man's inconsequentiality – a meditation that is in keeping
with the general meditation preceding prayer. (Letters from the
Rebbe, vol. 2, page 38).*

Guided imagery is a recognized therapeutic modality
that has successfully been used in many settings to benefit
patients suffering from a variety of conditions. It has been
shown, for example, to reduce pain and discomfort in
seriously injured burn patients as well as in women with
metastatic breast cancer, to improve mood in patients
suffering from depression and other mood disorders, to
boost the immune response in research subjects, and to
speed healing in patients who have just undergone surgery.

In her book, *Staying Well with Guided Imagery*,[175]
Belleruth Naparstek—a psychotherapist for over 25 years
and a pioneer in Guided Imagery—discusses the power

---

175 Belleruth Naparstek, *Staying Well with Guided Imagery* (New York: Wellness
Central, 1994), pp. 17-21.

of imagery to affect a person's health, both positively and negatively. According to Ms. Naparstek, "imagery" refers to any sensory experience that we have, whether visual, auditory, olfactory, gustatory, or tactile. These images—such as the smell of home-baked bread, the scent of our mother's cologne, the sound of leaves crunching underfoot as we walk through a park in late autumn—are "the true language of the body, the only language it understands immediately and without question."

"*Images are events to the Body.* Initially, most people make the mistake of thinking that imagery means something strictly visual. When I refer to imagery, I'm talking about *any perception that comes through any of the senses.* That means sights, sounds, smells, tastes, and feel. So, for instance, recalling the smell and feel of the air at the start of the first winter snowfall is an image....

These sensory images are the true language of the body, the only language it understands immediately and without question. To the body, these images can be almost as real as actual events. This is the first operating principle of imagery: *Our bodies don't discriminate between sensory images in the mind and what we call reality.* Although images don't have the same intense impact on the body that real events do, they elicit the same essential quality of experience in the body. It's a little bit like what an echo is to the sound that generated it, or perhaps a pastel version of bold original colors. With sensory image, echoes of the mood, emotions, physiological state, and blood chemistry associated with the original event reverberate in the body.

The good news, of course, is that we can deliberately introduce healthful images, and the gullible body will respond as if they, too, were approximations of reality. A spate of research findings shows the physical changes that can occur in the body as a result of such engineering with the imagination. A neuropsychologist at George Washington Medical Center, Nicholas Hall, found that his subjects could use imagery to increase the number of circulating white blood cells, as well as levels of thymosin-alpha-1, a hormone used by T helper cells....

Other studies show imagery to have a positive impact on depression... [and to] help people in difficult and physically challenging circumstances. At the University of Texas Health Science Center in Dallas, Cornelia Kenner and Jeanne Achterberg showed that seriously injured burn patients who used imagery experienced less pain and used less medication; in another study, with people on the orthopedic unit who had multiple fractures, this same team showed that imagery significantly helped alleviate their pain and anxiety.... Researchers from Papworth Hospital in Cambridge, England, found that patients who used guided imagery audiotapes during surgery recovered faster and left the hospital, on average, a day and a half earlier than other patients....

There is one study, however, by David Spiegal [sic], a psychiatrist at Stanford University, that measures the effects [of imagery] years later. Spiegal divided a group of eighty-six middle aged women with metastasized breast cancer into two groups. One group got state-of-the-art medical treatment only; the other received the same medical treatment, but along with it had weekly counseling sessions for one year, where they learned self-hypnosis and guided imagery. The imagery was simple. They imagined themselves floating gently on water, feeling relaxed and peaceful. That was it.

As was expected, after the year was up, the second group reported less pain and discomfort, fewer mood swings, a generally more optimistic outlook, and a greater feeling of being in control.... [T]en years later, Spiegal decided to check the death records of all eighty-six patients. Much to his surprise, he found that the second group had lived an average of twice as long as the first group (36.6 months [longer] versus 18.9 months).

The Power of the Altered State

The second key principle that makes guided imagery work is this: *In the altered state, we are capable of more rapid and intense healing, growth, learning, and change.* This is another one of those profound but simple truths that we have all experienced.

By altered state, I mean a relaxed focus, a kind of calm but energized alertness, a focused reverie. Attention is concentrated on one thing or a very narrow band of things."

Meditation, *hisbonenus*, helps us internalize what we have learned, to bring theory into practice. It is important to learn what many Chassidic masters have to teach us about the spiritual benefits of meditating. Throughout the Tanya the Rebbe emphasizes how important meditation is for self-refinement, and for its power to reveal the hidden love of G-d which each and every Jew has buried deep within himself.

Appendix C: Lovesickness

Based on Mystery of Marriage by Rabbi Yitzchak Ginsburgh

R' Akiva used to say:

Beloved is man for he was created in the image of G-d; an even greater expression of love is that it was made known to him that he was created in the image of G-d, as it is stated: "For in the image of G-d He made man."

Beloved are the people of Israel for they are called 'children of G-d'; an even greater expression of love is that it was made known to them that they are called the children of G-d, as it is said, "You are the children of G-d, your G-d."

Beloved are the people of Israel, for a precious article was given to them; an even greater expression of love is that it was made known to them that they were given a precious article, as it is said: "I have given you a good teaching, do not forsake My Torah" (Pirkei Avot Ch. 3:14 (18))

It is clear how much Hashem loves us, and that not only does He love us deeply and profoundly, but also that He makes this love known to us; not only does He make it known to us, but also does He give us His Torah and makes it known to us that He has given us His Torah because He loves us.

These three main categories of Hashem's love for us—being created in His image, being His children, and being given His precious Torah—relate to our typical daily experiences, personally and historically, as Jews. Rabbi Akiva, having experienced this himself, was able to summarize our history with these *pesukim*.

We know how cherished we are to Hashem. The word used in the first sentence, "adam," man, refers to all humans, every person created by Hashem.

This applies individually and generally.

Every human being is born with the potential for holiness.

When we become *bar* or *bat mitzvah*, we receive an additional measure of *kedushah*, of holiness, activating this latent potential. We are then capable of observing the Torah. This growth is reflected in R' Akiva's opening words:

"Beloved is man [from the time] he was created," yet it is not until one becomes *bar* or *bat mitzvah,* when the yetzer tov, the good inclination within us, is energized and our G-dly essence begins to develop. (Tanya) It is with this maturation that one is truly considered a Jew and not simply 'adam,' a person. As we grow and mature, we are increasingly able to internalize the teachings of the Torah, which benefits us and enables us to benefit others.

Historically, G-d created the world and all its inhabitants, then chose Avraham and the Jewish people to receive His Torah.

This is our daily practice: When we first arise in the morning, we re-experience being created in the image of Hashem; when we come close to Hashem through our prayers, we are like Hashem's child; as the day goes on, we grow to a level at which we can learn Torah, and we appreciate the gift that Hashem has given us.

This was Rabbi Akiva's experience: He was unlearned and descended from converts, yet as he aged he recognized the value of his being—that is, his Jewishness. He began to study how to be a Jew, starting at the very beginning. In his service of Hashem and study of His Torah, Akiva grew exceptionally close to Him and exceptionally wise.

Because of His love for us, Hashem gives us the ability every day to ascend to a high level of closeness to Him. The more we appreciate how much He loves us, the closer we can get. It's important to recognize how great His love for us truly is. Rabbi Ginsburg, in his book Mystery of Marriage (chapter one, pages 23-38) brings to light that G-d is, in fact, "lovesick" over us. He explores this "lovesickness" of G-d and our reaction to it, comparing the relationship between Hashem and the Jewish people to the five lovesick couples in our history. By examining their experience of lovesickness, we can learn how to follow G-d's ways and experience a lovesickness for Hashem. From there, we can increase our love for the Jewish people and, of course, our own spouse.

Analyzing different biblical relationships, you will see that sometimes one person takes the initiative and feels a greater love at first than their soon-to-be-spouse; sometimes the feeling is not mutual; sometimes both participants in the relationship have equally strong feelings. This information could help many people who are dating or even those who are further along in a relationship. It may be of great value to those at the stage of marrying off children.

Let's look at these couples: Adam and Chava (Eve), Yitzchak (Isaac) and Rivkah (Rebecca), Yaakov (Jacob) and Rochel (Rachel).

Adam, at first, was not happy with his partner Chava, because he had been awake to witness her being created from his ribs, and the sight disgusted him. Hashem saw that this was too much for Adam, so He caused him to sleep. When he awoke and saw her this time, the realization that this woman was 'the flesh of my flesh' brought forth feelings of love for her.

Rivkah had decided that she would marry Yitzchak even before meeting him. As soon as she saw Yitzchak, her feelings of love were so overwhelming that she almost fell off the camel she was riding. The very fact of her decision to marry Yitzchak was a process through which G d blessed her with falling in love with him. Yitzchak, on the other hand, did not let his guard come down until he took Rivkah into the tent and realized that she was k'Sarah, like Sarah. At that point, after they were married, he began to feel love for her.

The word "k'Sarah" also has the connotation of "kesherah, she is kosher." Yitzchak was uncertain if Rivkah was truly the pure soul she appeared to be. He knew that she came from a very dysfunctional, and possibly very evil, family. He therefore did not experience love for her until he saw the signs that reassured him of her purity.

Yaakov was so lovesick when he saw Rachel that he was empowered to move huge rocks on her behalf. He committed himself to a long period of servitude just on the promise that when it ended, she would marry him. And when it did end, and Rachel was denied him, he committed himself to another seven years of labor to finally be allowed to wed her.

Some relationships are based on love at first sight, in some relationships love develops from the commitment of being engaged, and in others, the emotion does not develop until after marriage.

"Lovesickness" factors into each of these paradigmatic relationships, but at different times and different levels. The discrepancy in timing is not because these holy couples were not destined to be together, or because they were not true soul mates. According to the Sages, the participants in these relationships were indeed soul mates and remain so through the ages.

Rabbi Ginsburg relates that because today, our souls have come back so many times in *gilgulim*, reincarnations, that when we do meet our soul mate again in this incarnation, we may not feel as excited as we would have the first time. The feeling that we have met our bashert, intended mate, can be less intense than we expect. This feeling may not occur until the engagement, or the wedding, or even a few years into the marriage. This strong love may need time to develop through giving and through shared experience.

Shlomo HaMelech (King Solomon) taught two contradictory concepts. In Proverbs (18:22) he teaches *Matza ishah matza tov,* "Who finds a wife, finds good," but in Ecclesiastes (7:26) he writes the opposite: *U'motze ani mar mimavet, et ha'ishah,* And I have found something more bitter than death, the woman." The *Gemara* (Berachot 8a) relates that in *Eretz Yisrael* when a man would marry, he would be asked, "*Matza* or *motze*? Did you find good, or bitterness?"

These opening words are so similar yet precede such different statements. The word *matza*, finds, represents the man who can say that he has found his spiritual essence, his other half, whom he knows to be a G-dly person in the image of Hashem. It's a done deal; he recognizes his wife's amazing qualities even while acknowledging that like anyone else, she might have some less-than perfect qualities too. The other verse, though, includes the word "ani", I. "I find women more bitter than death." *Motze* indicates that he is still looking, searching as if he can't find good yet. Basically, he only sees the negatives in his spouse; he has not yet connected to the fact that she is created in the image of G d and therefore is holy. The "I" represents the egotistical person who is in the relationship only for his own gratification. He has not been looking for the common soul root in the other person. Therefore, his relationship will always be bitter to him.

Love is about giving. Hashem, Who loves us and is lovesick for us, at whatever stage we are in life, is constantly giving to us. In fact, every Shabbat His lovesickness for us is ignited anew, and we experience its development throughout the week. On Shabbat, Hashem gives us an extra soul--His seed of love. With that seed of love, just as with a seed of pregnancy, a gestation period follows, during which we take action to keep the fetus healthy; we eat right, sleep right, exercise, and take our vitamins. So too, we take that revelation of love from Hashem and develop it further to an even greater level of love. Then because of our efforts Hashem in turn, becomes even more lovesick over us.

On Shabbat, if we pray and learn and say *Tehillim*, and try our best to keep the laws of the holy day, if we try to speak with proper words, and not discuss mundane topics, the holiness of the day will increase. That ignites Hashem's love for us and it will overflow into the following week.

Every week we repeat this experience, and every week Hashem's lovesickness for us is reignited. Shabbat is called a "*klei chemdah*, a vessel of delight": Hashem has given us the ability to delight in Him loving us. Imagine one person saying to another, "I love you! What can I do for you? Let me bring you a glass of water. Can I shine your shoes? Anything, I will do anything for you." And the other person isn't even interested, imagine they are looking away, their facial expression bored. The first person is willing to do so much for the one he loves, but the other is so cold, so uncaring.

Hashem is running to us, offering us everything, saying "I love you, I love you." Knowing now how lovesick and beloved we are to Him, can arouse in us a sense of appreciation for His love, so that we feel a greater joy in reciprocating that love.

How different Shabbat will be, now that we understand this! How different our everyday *tefillah* and Torah learning will be. This scenario should be ingrained in our hearts and in our minds because so many of us, so often, feel that we are not good enough for Hashem or are not doing enough for Hashem or His creations. We feel that we have failed G-d and therefore, feel we feel dejected, and in our pain, we make erroneous calculations. We think that Hashem does not love us, and that this or that happened "because G-d doesn't love me." But that is not true.

In *Parshat Shelach* we read the episode of the spies, were sent to report on the conditions in *Eretz Yisrael*. They saw a beautiful, fruitful land, but because they had such a dejected view of themselves, they could not accept it as their own. The spies described themselves as being "like grasshoppers" compared to the inhabitants of the land. They believed that they could not succeed in taking over the land; they could not believe that they were worthy of Hashem's special care.

The more dejected and lowly they felt in their own eyes, the less they were stuck and not able to move forward. The spies had witnessed so many miracles from Egypt into the wilderness, but they could not accept that these miracles would continue after the people of Israel would enter Eretz Yisrael. In the wilderness, the Jews led a very spiritual existence: the manna was edible with no effort on their part beyond picking it up; their shoes did not wear out; their clothing did not get dirty, shrink, or rip; there was no labor required for any of their physical needs. Hashem's presence was obvious.

But the spies realized that this would change when they entered *Eretz Yisrael*. The people would have to toil for their every need. They would have to work the land. From being suffused with the spiritual, they would become immersed in the material.

Given the more physical existence, the spies wondered if Hashem would continue to love them as He did in the desert. How could He respect them, now that they were all such mundane people? Would Hashem still feel attached to them and make miracles for them? That was the dilemma of the spies. They could not fathom G d being so close to them even in their down times. And that is where they went wrong.

We have to *"matza tov,"* find the good in ourselves. We have to recognize and accept our G-dly essence. G d loves us, period. Understanding this and tapping into it, we can rise above the natural order and develop a closer relationship with Hashem. When we are secure in our relationship to Hashem, we can be calm and settled, able to move forward with a greater speed. Whether we are up, down, or sideways, we are guaranteed that He does miracles for us and will continue to do so. In fact, when G d is involved in our lives in the natural order of things, it's even more miraculous. It's one thing for a Jew to see the splitting of the sea—it's amazing, overwhelming, breathtaking! But His providing our sustenance through a livelihood, and making sure that bread is on our table, is even more miraculous.

Rebbe Rashab, (*Kuntras Uma'ayan*, chapter, 28 page 142) What is the meaning of the verse (Joel 3:18), *"And from the wellsprings of the Lord, Hashem will water the valley of Shittim"*? Even when a person is "in the valley," pulled down by the *"ruach shtus,"* the spirit of folly, and ensnared there by the *yetzer hara*, Hashem will provide for him water from the wellsprings of the Torah. G-d Himself will make sure you have water for your soul; He will help you out of the valley.

We learn that Hashem is lovesick over us. He wants only good for us and never, *chas ve'shalom,* the opposite. G-d is an all-consuming G-d and He has an "all-consuming fire". We often do not realize what a fiery, passionate love He feels for us. This love can warm us, and ignite a reciprocal love for Him. With our recognition of His love, we feel loving and fiery and vital and lively and excited, and able to serve Hashem with a similarly passionate emotion that will spill over into every good we do.

We should ponder G-d's love for us not only on Shabbat, but every day. He empowers us to reignite the love for our spouse, for our children, for *Am Yisrael,* and for ourselves.

Imagine a woman watching an artist fashioning a masterpiece; as he works, the woman admires his hands and praises his genius, his talent, and his skill. The artist basks in the compliments. So too when we look at G-d's creations--including ourselves!--and we find our Divine essence. We must know we have been created in the image of Hashem, and see ourselves in this positive way. Then Hashem will be gratified and excited that we appreciate His creation.

It is a wonderful cycle of *kedushah,* holiness, as we receive and create increasing amounts of appreciation, positivity, and love.

Recent understanding of workings our our mind show that the the brain has the power to create new pathways by shedding old, under used neurons. This process is called neural (or synaptic) pruning. In simple layman terms, when the brain is used more often to think of positive thoughts, (I.e. focusing on Hashem's all-encompassing love and care and concern for us,) and avoiding negative thoughts, the negative thoughts then are discarded and become obsolete. This in turn frees our mind up for more positivity. As a result, you feel physiologically better, too, because a more positive mind set leads to a happy mind, which leads to a healthy body. Negative thoughts lead to anxiety and tension which may have a debilitating effect on one's overall health.

In the TED Global Talk "How to Make Stress Your Friend," (Sept. 4, 2013), therapist Kelly McGonigal related that originally, her professional goal was to help people get rid of the stress in their lives. She thought and taught that "stress was the enemy," the cause of every ailment from hangnails to heart disease. But one day she discovered a long-term study on the effects of stress that changed her entire outlook. The study (which tracked 30,000 people for eight years) concluded that the effect stress has on a person depends on how that person relates to the stress. The study compared three groups: those who view stress as a good motivator that influences them to be efficient and competent; those who see stress as horrific and crippling, and those who said they had no particular stress in their lives. The results showed the highest rate of death in the years they covered, in the second group. The first group, those who viewed stress positively, had the lowest rate of death and the lowest incidence of health concerns, even compared to those who claimed they didn't experience stress. McGonigal was asked whether it was necessarily better to choose a non-stressful job over an obviously stressful one. She answered that one should choose the job that presents a more meaningful opportunity, even if appears to be more stressful, because "chasing meaning is better for your health than trying to avoid discomfort."

So try your best to focus on the positive in every situation, and ultimately you will be more productive, happy and healthy.

Hashem loves you endlessly, like a child in a parent's old age; Please do your best to always keep this in the forefront of your mind and remember that Hashem is actually lovesick over you.

May we all be blessed to have an ever more delightful relationship with Hashem, and with His people.

Let us follow His lead and let us make known to the people in our lives how much we love them. And we, too, will reach new heights.

Recommended Reading

For women:

Women in the Talmud, by Judith Abrams

Women in the Holocaust, by Dalia Ofer and Lenore J. Weitzman

Women's Wisdom, by Rabbi Shalom Arush

In Her Own Right ... A Great Woman: Rebbetzin Rivkah, Wife of the Rebbe Maharash (Fourth Lubavitcher Rebbe), by Malka Schwartz

Through You, Israel Will Be Blessed, by Malka Schwartz

For men:

The Garden of Peace, by Rabbi Shalom Arush

For both men and women:

To Love and To Cherish, by Rabbi Shalom Arush

As A Father Loves His Only Son, Talks of the Lubavitcher Rebbe, Rabbi Menachem M. Schneerson on Bitachon: Trusting in G-d.

Bibliography

Aaron, Rabbi David. *Seeing G-d: Ten Life-Changing Lessons of the Kabbalah*. New York: Penguin Group (USA) Inc., 2000.

Baal Shem Tov, Rabbi Israel. *Tzava'at Harivash*, translated and annotated by J. Immanuel Schochet. New York: Kehot Publication Society, 1998.

Bogomilsky, Rabbi Moshe. *Vedibarta Bum: Rosh Hashana, Yom Kippur, and Sukkot*. Merkos Linyonei Chinuch, Brooklyn, New York, 2006.

Dalfin, Rabbi Chaim. *The Rebbe's Advice*. New York: Mendelsohn, 1997.

Feuer, Rabbi Avrohom Chaim. *ArtScroll Tanach Series Tehillim*, Vol 2. New York: Mesorah Publications, Ltd, 2002.

Feuer, Rabbi Avrohom Chaim. *Iggeres HaRamban: A Letter for the Ages*. New York: Mesorah Publications, Ltd, 1989.

Ginsburgh, Rabbi Yitzchak. *The Mystery of Marriage*. Kfar Chabad, Israel: Gal Einai, 1999.

Glatt, Rabbi Aaron Eli, M.D. *Women in the Talmud*. New York: Mesorah Publications, Ltd, 2003.

Jacobson, Rabbi Simon. *60 Days*. New York: Kiyum Press 2003.

Kahn, Rabbi Rafael Nachman. *Extraordinary Chassidic Tales*, Vol 3. New York, Jerusalem: Otsar Sifrei Lubavitch, Inc., 1999.

Kalmenson, Rabbi Mendel. *Seeds of Wisdom: Based on Personal Encounters With the Rebbe* New York: Jewish Educational Media, 2013.

Klapholz, Rabbi Yisroel Yaakov. *Stories of the Bal Shem Tov*. New York: Mishor Publishing Co. Ltd, 1989.

Majeski, Rabbi Shloma. *The Chassidic Approach to Joy*. New York: Sichos In English, 1995.

Miller, Rabbi Chaim. *The Gutnick Edition Chumash*. New York: Kol Menachem, 2004.

Naparstek, Belleruth. *Staying Well With Guided Imagery*. New York, Boston: Wellness Central, 1994.

Nelson, Dr. Bradley. *The Emotion Code*. Mesquite, Nevada: Wellness Unmasked Publishing, 2007.

Pinson, Rabbi DovBer. *Reincarnation and Judaism: The Journey of the Soul*. New Jersey: Jason Aronson, Inc., 1999.

Pliskin, Rabbi Zelig. *Kindness*. New York: Mesorah Publication, Ltd, 2000.

Schneerson, Rabbi Menachem Mendel, *HaYom Yom*. New York: Sichos in English, 2009.

—*Letters From the Rebbe*. New York: Otsar Sifrei Lubavitch, Inc.,

Schneersohn, Rabbi Shalom DovBer. *Forces in Creation*. New York: Kehot Publication Society, 2003.

—*The Power of Return*. New York: Kehot Publication Society, 2005.

Schneersohn, Rabbi Yosef Yitzchak . *Likkutei Dibburim*, Vol 1-5. New York: Kehot Publication Society, 2000.

Wineberg, Rabbi Yosef. *Lessons in Tanya*.Vol 1-5. New York: Kehot Publication Society, 2001.

About the Author

Miriam Yerushalmi holds an M.S. in Psychology and Marriage and Family Counseling. Trained at Pepperdine University (graduation 1990). Miriam works in private practice with families and children, including volunteering many hours providing a resource for the neediest to access appropriate Mental Health care.

Miriam is uniquely skilled at combining behavioral and humanistic approaches to address a wide spectrum of psychopathology. From panic disorders to addiction to depressive disorders, anxiety, anger management and ADHD, Miriam imparts self regulation techniques where clients learn to develop tools for a balanced and fulfilled life.

Miriam is a sought after speaker who lectures internationally and has over 250 audio classes available. She writes regularly for the Jewish Press, lectures for Torah Anytime and has presented workshops at the annual *Nefesh* conference for therapists. Since 2014 she began working for SPARKS as a counselor, in addition giving teleconferences and webinars on the topic of overcoming stress and anxiety as well as writing articles for their magazine called "True Balance" and other duties. She continues to teach a weekly class in the central synagogue in Crown Heights, NY (770) as well as in Long Island, each of which started over 15 years ago.

Miriam Yerushalmi fuses essential Torah principles with her background in Mental Health to empower individuals to release their inner healing potential while aligning with life's purpose on essential life issues, ranging from relationships and parenting to self improvement.

CPSIA information can be obtained
at www.ICGtesting.com
Printed in the USA
BVOW03*1446120817
491733BV00010B/26/P